ESTINE
THE ADVENTURES OF MIGUEL LITTÍN
CHILE

Gabriel García Márquez
Translated by Asa Zatz

An Owl Book / Henry Holt and Company / New York

Henry Holt and Company, Inc.
Publishers since 1866
115 West 18th Street
New York, New York 10011

Henry Holt ® is a registered
trademark of Henry Holt and Company, Inc.

Published in Canada by Fitzhenry & Whiteside Ltd.,
195 Allstate Parkway, Markham, Ontario L3R 4T8.

Library of Congress Cataloging-in-Publication Data
García Márquez, Gabriel, 1928–
Clandestine in Chile.
Translation of: La aventura de Miguel Littín,
clandestino en Chile.
1. Chile—Politics and government—1970– 2. Chile—Description
and travel—1981– 3. Littín, Miguel. 4. Moving-picture
producers and directors—Chile—Biography. I. Littín, Miguel.
II. Title
F3100.G37513 1987   983'.064   87-39

ISBN 0-8050-0322-3
ISBN 0-8050-0945-0 (An Owl Book: pbk.)

Henry Holt books are available for special promotions
and premiums. For details contact: Director, Special Markets.

Originally published in Colombia under the title
La aventura de Miguel Littín, clandestino en Chile.

First published in hardcover in 1987 by
Henry Holt and Company, Inc.

First Owl Book Edition—1988

Designed by Susan Hood

Printed in the United States of America
All first editions are printed on acid-free paper.∞

10 9 8 7 6 5 4 3

CLANDESTINE IN CHILE

Far-ranging bird, aloft
you seemed
suspended
between continents
over lost seas;
a flick
of a wing,
a bell clap
of feathers:
majestically, you changed
your course a fraction
and, triumphant and true,
continued on your implacable,
lonely
route.

CLAND IN

Hero, I said; no one
will erect
on the soil
of some public plaza
your inspiring
statue,
no one.
Instead, amid
somber official laurels
will be installed
a mustached man
in frock coat or with sword,
a man who killed
a peasant woman
in the war,
a man who with a single
bloody shell
demolished
a school for
little girls,
a man who usurped
the Indians'
lands,
a hunter
of doves,
exterminator
of black swans. . . .

don't expect
them to erect
a monument
to your feats;
and while
melancholy spectators
gathered around your remains,
plucking
a feather,
a petal, a message
from a hurricane,
I walked away,
so that
at least
your memory,
without a stone, without a statue,
might on these lines fly
for the last time into
space,
and your flight stay close to the sea.

Miguel Littín before entering Chile.

Disguised as a Uruguayan businessman in Santiago.

Introduction

Early in 1985, the Chilean film director Miguel Littín—
whose name was on a list of 5,000 exiles absolutely forbidden
to return to their country—spent six weeks in Chile, through
the art of personal disguise and deception. There he shot over
100,000 feet of film about the state of his country after twelve
years of military dictatorship. He entered Chile on a false
passport. Makeup artists had altered his face and he spoke
and dressed in the manner of a successful Uruguayan businessman. Protected by underground resistance groups, Littín
traveled the length and breadth of the country, directing
three European film crews (who had entered Chile legally
on various film assignments), as well as six young film crews
from the Chilean resistance. They even shot footage inside
President Pinochet's private office. The result was a four-
hour film for television and a two-hour feature for movie
theaters now beginning to be shown around the world.

Early in 1986 in Madrid, when Miguel Littín told me what
he had done and how he had done it, I realized that behind
his film there was another film that would probably never

be made. And so he agreed to a grueling interrogation, the tape of which ran some eighteen hours. It encompassed the full human adventure in all its professional and political implications, which I have condensed into ten chapters.

Some of the names have been changed and many of the circumstances altered to protect those involved who are still in Chile. I preferred to keep Littín's story in the first person, to preserve its personal—and sometimes confidential—tone, without any dramatic additions or historical pretentiousness on my part. The manner of the final text is, of course, my own, since a writer's voice is not interchangeable, particularly when he has to condense almost 600 pages into less than 200. Notwithstanding, I have tried to keep the Chilean idioms of the original and, in all cases, to respect the narrator's way of thinking, which does not always coincide with mine.

In its nature and its method of disclosure, this is a piece of reporting. Yet it is something more: the emotional reconstruction of an adventure the finality of which was unquestionably much more visceral and moving than the original—and effectively realized—intention of making a film that made fun of the dangers of military power. Littín himself said, "This may not have been the most heroic action of my life, but it is the most worthwhile." It is, and I believe that therein lies its greatness.

—*Gabriel García Márquez*

CLANDESTINE IN CHILE

Oh, dark captain,
defeated in my country,
may your proud
wings
still soar above
the final wave, the wave of death.

—Pablo Neruda
from "Ode to the Voyager Albatross"

Translated from the Spanish by
Margaret Peden

1

Miguel Littín
Clandestine in Chile

Ladeco flight 115 from Asunción, Paraguay, was about to land an hour late at Santiago's Pudahuel airport. Aconcagua, to the left, was, at 23,000 feet, a steel promontory in the moonlight. The plane dipped its left wing with terrifying grace, leveled off with a lugubrious creaking of metal, and landed prematurely in three kangaroo hops. I, Miguel Littín, son of Hernán and Cristina, and a film director, was home after twelve years of exile, though still exiled within myself, for I came with a false identity, a false passport, even a false wife. My face and appearance were so altered by makeup and unfamiliar clothing that even close friends would fail to recognize me in broad daylight some days later.

Very few people in the world knew my secret and one of them was on the plane with me. She was Elena, a young, attractive activist, designated by her Chilean resistance organization to act as liaison for me with the underground network, make secret contacts, decide the most appropriate meeting places, appraise the operational situations, arrange appointments, and see to our safety. Though she lived in

1

Europe, she frequently traveled to Chile on political missions like this one. In case I was discovered by the police, disappeared, or failed to make prearranged contacts on schedule, she was to spread the news of my presence in Chile to touch off an international alarm. Although our identity papers showed no marital connection, we had traveled as a loving couple from Madrid halfway around the world through seven airports. However, on this last leg of our flight from Rio de Janeiro by way of Paraguay, we had decided to sit apart and to disembark as strangers. Our fear was that Chilean immigration security would be so tight at the airport that I might be found out immediately. If that happened, Elena would then go through immigration alone and notify her underground organization. If we passed through security undetected, we would revert to being a couple at the airport exit.

Our idea sounded very simple on paper, but proved to be risky in practice. The plan was to film an underground documentary on the increasingly desperate situation in Chile after twelve years of General Augusto Pinochet's dictatorship. I had been unable to get the idea of making this film out of my mind. I had lost the image of my country in a fog of nostalgia. The Chile I remembered no longer existed, and for a filmmaker there could be no surer way of rediscovering a lost country than by going back to it and filming it from the inside. In 1983 the dream grew more persistent as the Chilean government began publishing lists of exiles who would be allowed to return. But my name did not appear on any of them. The dream reached a pitch of desperation later, when the Chilean government published the list of 5,000 names of those who could still not come back and this time my name was among them. When the plan to enter Chile illegally took shape as a reality, almost by chance and unexpectedly, I had already given up on it more than two years before.

By the fall of 1984 I had settled in the Basque city of San

Sebastián with my wife, Ely, and our three children to make a feature film which, like so many others in the secret history of the movies, was canceled by the producers only a week before shooting was scheduled to begin. I was suddenly idle and the old idea of making the film about Chile came back to me. At dinner in a local restaurant one night, I mentioned my dream to some friends. The idea was discussed at the table with much interest, not only for its obvious political implications, but because each of us reveled in the notion of thumbing our noses at Pinochet. But nobody seemed to take it for anything more than an exile's brainstorm. On our way home, however, through the sleeping streets of the old city, the Italian producer Luciano Balducci, who had said scarcely a word at the table, took me by the arm and drew me aside in an apparently casual manner.

"The man you need," he said to me, "is waiting in Paris."

It was true. The man I needed was high up in the Chilean resistance and his plan differed from mine only in certain minor aspects. Some months later in Paris, one four-hour conversation in the lively café atmosphere of La Coupole, with Balducci's enthusiastic participation, was enough to bring to reality a fantasy I had hatched complete with its smallest details during the chimerical sleeplessness of exile.

The first step was to bring three film crews into Chile: one Italian, one French, and one of mixed nationality, but with Dutch credentials. Everything was to be done legally. Each crew would enter Chile with legitimate credentials and prearranged permits and each would establish contact with its respective embassy. The cover for the Italian crew, headed by a newspaperwoman, was to be the filming of a documentary on Chile's Italian immigrants, particularly Joaquino Toesca, the architect of the Moneda Palace. The French crew was to be authorized to make an ecological film on the geography of Chile, and the third crew to do a study on its recent earthquakes. No crew would be aware of the existence

3

of the other two. No member of any of the crews would know in advance what the true purpose of the filming was or that it was I who was directing from behind the scenes, except for the person in charge of each group, who had to be a recognized professional in the field, to have a political background, and to be fully aware of the risks involved. I managed to arrange this with one short visit to the country of origin of each group. Before I arrived in Chile, the three film crews, formally authorized and with their contracts in order, were already there awaiting instructions, ready to begin filming immediately. That was the easiest part.

The Drama of Becoming Somebody Else

Becoming another person was the hardest part, more difficult than I could have imagined. Changing personality is a daily battle in which, wishing to continue being ourselves, we keep rebelling against our own determination to change. And so, the main difficulty was not the learning process, as might be expected, but my unconscious resistance to change, in body and behavior. I had to resign myself to giving up being the man I had always been and transform myself into another, different one, above the suspicion of the same repressive police who had forced me out of my country. I had to become unrecognizable even to my friends. Two psychologists and a movie makeup expert, under the direction of a specialist in clandestine operations sent from Chile, brought off the miracle in a little less than three weeks, relentlessly resisting my instinctive determination to go on being me.

The first thing to go was my beard. This was not just a simple matter of shaving. The beard had created a personality for me that I now had to shed. I had grown my first beard as a young man, before making my first film, and although I shaved it a number of times since, I was never without it when filming. It was as though a beard were an inseparable part of my identity as a film director. My uncles had worn beards and no doubt that increased the allure of beards for me. I had shaved mine off in Mexico a few years before but never managed to get my friends and family, much less myself, to accept my new face. All had the impression of being with an impostor, but I persisted in remaining clean-shaven for a few weeks because I thought I looked younger that way. It was my youngest daughter, Catalina, who clinched it for me.

"You do look younger without the beard," she told me, "but uglier, too."

So my teachers snipped it off little by little, observing the effect of the various cuts on my appearance and personality, until finally I was clean-shaven. It was several days before I could work up the courage to look in the mirror.

Next was the hair on my head. Mine is pitch-black, inherited from a Greek mother and a Palestinian father who also passed on to me my tendency to premature baldness. The first thing the makeup experts did was to dye it light brown. Then, after combing it in various styles, they ended up not fighting nature. Instead of covering my bald spot, as was first planned, they enlarged it, not just by combing the hair straight back but by finishing with tweezers what the years had begun.

It is hard to believe how almost imperceptible touches can change one's facial structure. I have a moon face even when I weigh less than I did at that time, but after the ends of my eyebrows had been plucked, my face seemed longer. The change made me look more Oriental, in fact, closer to how I ought to have looked, considering my ancestry.

The last step was prescription lenses, which gave me a severe headache for the first few days I wore them. But eventually they changed not only the shape of my eyes but their expression as well. After weeks of a beggarly diet I shed twenty pounds and the physical transformation was complete.

Metamorphosis of the body was easy but demanded greater concentration, because here I had to accept a change in economic class. Instead of my habitual jeans and leather jacket, I had to get used to suits of British cloth, made-to-measure shirts, suede shoes, and florid Italian ties. Instead of my brusque, Chilean country accent, I had to assume the rhythm of a wealthy Uruguayan, the handiest nationality for my new identity. I had to learn to laugh differently, to walk slowly, and to use my hands for emphasis when I spoke. In short, I had to give up being the casual, nonconformist film director I had always been and transform myself into what I wanted least in the world to be: a smug bourgeois or, as we say in Chile, a *momio*.*

"Laugh and You're Dead"

At the same time that I was being transformed into somebody else, I was also learning to live with Elena in a 16th-century Arrondissement house in Paris. It was not my house, and it was unlike any place I had ever lived. Yet I had to create memories of it to avoid possible contradictions in the future. It was one of the strangest experiences of my life, because I realized that although Elena was charming and would be no less so in intimate life, I never could have lived with her. She had been selected by experts for her professional experience and her political credentials, to keep me on a short leash with no slack for indulging my bent for improvisation. As a film director, I did not take kindly to that. Later on, after all had turned out well, I would recognize that I had done

Momio: a person so resistant to change that he might as well be dead— a mummy.

6

her an injustice because I had, in a subconscious way, judged her according to the disguise we had both adopted. Recalling that strange experience now, I wonder if ours wasn't the perfect parody of a contemporary marriage: we could hardly stand being under the same roof together.

Elena had no identity problems. She is Chilean, although she hadn't lived in Chile regularly for over fifteen years. Since she was neither exiled nor wanted by the police anywhere in the world, her cover was perfect. She had carried out many important political missions in various countries and was intrigued by the idea of making a clandestine film in her own country. I was the difficult case. Pretending to be Uruguayan, which for technical reasons seemed the most appropriate nationality for me to assume, obliged me to adopt a character different from my own and to invent a past in a country I didn't know. Nevertheless, by the scheduled date, I had learned to react instantly on hearing my assumed name and was able to answer the most arcane questions about the city of Montevideo. I knew the bus lines I had to take to get home, and I could even tell ancient anecdotes about fellow students at High School No. 11 on Avenida Italiana, two blocks from a well-known drugstore and one block from a recently opened supermarket. The only thing I had to avoid was laughing, because my laugh was so characteristic that it could give me away despite my disguise. To impress this on me, the person in charge of my identity change warned me in the most ominous tone he could muster: "Laugh and you're dead." Of course, there was nothing out of the ordinary about a stone-faced international business tycoon.

During my training, an unforeseen problem arose: Pinochet declared a new state of siege. The experiments in a free market economy by the Chicago School, acting at the invitation of the government, had been a spectacular flop in Chile. The severe economic hardships that followed united the many and various resistance groups into a solid force for the first time. Even the most progressive sectors of the bourgeoisie joined the opposition forces, legal and illegal, in a one-day nationwide work stoppage. It was a display of power and determination that enraged Pinochet and brought on the state of siege.

"If this continues, we will have to have another eleventh of September," Pinochet threatened, in an ironic reference to the day in 1973 when he had toppled Salvador Allende's government in the midst of economic chaos.

The state of siege would appear to have favored the making of a film like ours, which would try to show the less obvious aspects of life inside Chile. However, there would be much stricter surveillance now, bloodier repression and shorter working hours, owing to the curfew. The internal resistance people weighed all the factors and decided to go ahead. We set out on the appointed day.

A Long Donkey's Tail for Pinochet

My first test was the day of departure from Madrid airport. I had not seen Ely or the children, Pochi, Miguelito, and Catalina, during the many weeks that it took to transform me into another man. The consensus had been that I should leave without notifying them in order to avoid the havoc of good-byes. At the beginning we thought it would be best for everybody if my family were not told about the project. However, we soon realized that this would not work. For one thing, nobody would be more helpful in the rearguard than Ely. She would be the ideal person to travel between Madrid and Paris, Paris and Rome, and even to Buenos Aires to receive and process the film I would be sending out from Chile. Also, she could raise additional money if needed.

When I returned to Madrid to make the last preparations before leaving, my children began to notice the changes. In my bedroom Catalina found the new clothing that was com-

8

pletely out of keeping with my normal way of dressing. Her uneasiness and curiosity were such that I had no choice but to bring the children together and let them in on the whole story. They listened with delight and a sense of complicity, as if they had suddenly become part of one of the films we often invented for our own amusement. When they saw me in the airport, transformed into a rather clerical-looking Uruguayan, however, they realized, as did I, that this film would be a real-life drama, as important as it was dangerous. Yet they were unanimous in their support and even made a game out of it.

"The important thing," they said, "is for you to pin a great long donkey's tail on Pinochet," referring to the party game in which blindfolded children try to pin a tail on a paper donkey.

"That's a promise," I told them, calculating the amount of film I intended to shoot. "It will be a tail about 20,000 feet long."

A week later Elena and I landed in Santiago. The trip had been an improvised pilgrimage through seven European cities in order to accustom me to handling my new identity. My passport bore the real name and description of a Uruguayan who had given it to us as a political contribution in the knowledge that it was to be used for entering Chile. All we did was substitute his photograph with one of me taken after my transformation. My shirts, attaché case, visiting cards, and stationery bore the name or initials of the passport owner. After hours of practice I had learned to execute his signature without hesitation. There wasn't the time to arrange for credit cards, possibly a dangerous omission since it was hardly conceivable that the man I was portraying would be paying for airplane tickets in cash.

Despite all the incompatibilities that would have immediately led to a divorce in real life, Elena and I had learned to act as though ours was a marriage capable of weathering the

9

stormiest domestic crisis. We had created a shared past for ourselves, complete with incidents, anecdotes, assumed habits and tastes, and then committed it all to memory. We had handled our assignment so conscientiously that I doubt we would have made a serious slip even under a thorough interrogation. Our cover story was foolproof. We were the directors of an advertising agency with headquarters in Paris, on our way to shoot a promotional picture for a new perfume to be launched on the European market the following autumn. We had selected Chile for the filming because it was one of the few countries where it was possible at any time of the year to find scenery corresponding to the four seasons and ranging from tropical beaches to perpetual snows. Elena, carrying herself with admirable self-assurance in her expensive European clothes, bore no resemblance to the young woman with long hair, plaid skirt, and schoolgirl loafers I had met in Paris. I too was feeling quite at home in my businessman's shell until I passed a showcase window, caught sight of my reflection in the glass, and, away from the house and the tutors, recognized how much I had become someone else. "How revolting!" I thought. "If I weren't I, I'd be just like that character." At that moment, all I had left of my former identity was a tattered copy of *The Lost Steps*, Alejo Carpentier's great novel, which I have carried in my luggage on all my trips for the last fifteen years to help ease my fear of flying. On top of that, I had to suffer my way past immigration windows in various airports of the world to get over my nervousness about the false passport.

My first experience was in Geneva. Everything went normally but I will never forget the ordeal. The immigration officer checked through the passport carefully, almost page by page, and then looked at my face to compare it with the one in the photograph. I was so nervous that I had to hold my breath as I looked at him, even though the photograph was my only legitimate connection to that passport. I did not experience that nausea and that heart-pounding anxiety again until the door of the plane opened at the airport in Santiago and I felt for the first time in twelve years the glacial air of the Andes. There was a large sign on the façade of the airport building that said: *Chile Advances in Order and Peace.* I looked at my watch. There was less than an hour to curfew.

2

First Disillusionment: The City's Magnificence

When the immigration officer opened my passport, I knew that if he were to look into my eyes he would discover my deception. There were three counters, all attended by men in uniform. I had decided to pick the youngest because he seemed to be working the fastest. Elena got into another line as though we were strangers so that if one of us ran into a problem, the other could sound the alarm. It was not necessary, though, because the immigration officers were as eager to avoid the curfew as the passengers and were barely glancing at our documents. The one who took care of me did not even stop to check my papers since Uruguayans are not required to have visas. He stamped the entry on the first clean page he came to and on returning the passport looked me full in the eyes with a directness that momentarily chilled me.

"Thank you," I said in a firm voice.

"Welcome to Chile," he answered, flashing a broad smile at me.

The luggage arrived with a speed that would have been

remarkable in the most modern airport in the world. I picked up my suitcase, then Elena's—we had decided that I would go out first with the luggage to gain time—and carried them to the customs platform. The officer there, as worried as everybody else about the curfew, was hurrying the travelers along instead of going through the luggage. As I was lifting mine to the counter, he asked, "Traveling alone?"

I said that I was. He gave the two suitcases a cursory glance. "Okay, move on." But a shout came from behind me: "Check that one." It was a woman supervisor I hadn't noticed until then, a classic tough type, blonde and masculine, in a double-breasted uniform. Not until that moment had it occurred to me that I couldn't explain why I had a suitcase full of women's clothes. Also, I couldn't believe that the supervisor had singled me out of all those passengers for nothing more serious than my luggage. While the man poked through my clothes, she asked for my passport and examined it closely. Knowing they would ask questions and fearing that my pseudo-Uruguayan accent might not conceal my Chilean identity, I popped a piece of hard candy into my mouth. The first question came from the man.

"How long will you be staying in Chile, sir?"

"Just long enough," I mumbled.

With the candy in my mouth, I myself couldn't make out what I was saying, but the man didn't seem to care and asked me to open the other bag. It was locked. Not knowing what to do, I looked around for Elena and found her still in the immigration line, standing stolidly, unaware of the tragedy that was brewing so close to her. I was about to declare her the owner of the suitcase without considering the consequences of my panicked decision, when the supervisor returned my passport and proceeded to someone else's suitcase. I turned to look for Elena again but couldn't find her. For the first time I realized how much I needed her, not just at this particular moment but for our entire adventure.

13

It was a magical phenomenon that we couldn't explain: Elena had become invisible. Later, she told me that while on line she had seen me taking her suitcase and thought it risky, but had relaxed when she saw me leave customs. I crossed the almost deserted waiting room, following a porter who had put our bags on his cart, and there I felt the first shock of my return.

I could see no evidence of the militarization I had anticipated, nor even any signs of poverty. True, this was not the vast, gloomy Los Cerrillos airport, from which I had set out on my exile on a rainy October night twelve years before, with a dreadful sense of the world disintegrating around me, but the modern Pudahuel airport, where I had been only once before the military coup. Yet it was not just a subjective impression. None of the armed presence one would have expected, particularly under the state of siege, was visible anywhere. The airport was clean and brightly lit wherever I looked, with colorful advertisements and big shops full of imported merchandise. There wasn't even the regular guard on duty for lost travelers. The taxis at the platform outside weren't the usual dilapidated old hulks, but late-model Japanese cars neatly lined up in a straight line.

But this was not the moment to be jumping to conclusions. The bags were stowed in a taxi, the hour of curfew was getting alarmingly close, and Elena was nowhere to be seen. Now I had another problem. According to our rules, if one of us should be left behind, the other was to go on and leave a message at the emergency telephone numbers we had been given. Yet I didn't want to leave by myself, especially since we had not yet decided on a hotel. I had written "El Conquistador" on the entry form as our address because it is a hotel commonly used by business people. Furthermore, I knew that our Italian film crew would be staying there, although I wasn't sure that Elena did.

Trembling with anxiety and the cold, I was on the point of giving up when I saw her running in my direction, pursued by a man in civilian clothes with a dark coat in his hand. I stood there petrified, preparing myself for the worst, when he caught up with her and handed over her raincoat, which she had forgotten in customs. She had been delayed there when the same woman customs inspector I had tangled with noticed that Elena was traveling without luggage and went through everything in her handbag, from identity papers to toilet articles.

She could not have imagined, of course, that the little Japanese transistor radio in Elena's bag was also a sort of weapon, our only means of contact with the internal resistance. I was more upset than Elena because I thought she had been missing for over half an hour, although she assured me it had been only six minutes. Finally we were able to relax when we learned from the driver that it was not twenty minutes but an hour and twenty minutes to curfew. My watch was still on Rio de Janeiro time. In Santiago it was 10:40 and the night was freezing cold.

Is This What I Came For?

As we approached the city, the joy of my return slowly gave way to a feeling of uncertainty. The route to the old Los Cerrillos airport was an avenue that went past rundown factories and through poor barrios that suffered brutal repression at the time of the coup. The new Pudahuel airport, however, lies on an expressway with a modern lighting system and that was a bad start for someone like me who, convinced of the evil of the dictatorship, needed to see clear evidence of its failures in the streets, in daily life, and in people's behavior, all of which could be filmed and shown to the world. But now my disquiet gave way to frank disappointment. Elena later confessed to me that although she had been back to Chile a number of times in recent years, she too felt similarly disturbed.

This was not easily dismissed. Contrary to what we had heard in exile, Santiago was a radiant city, its venerable monuments splendidly illuminated, its streets spotlessly clean and orderly. If anything, armed policemen were more in evidence on the streets of Paris or New York than here. Starting at the historic Central Station, designed by the same Gustave Eiffel who built the tower in Paris, the endless Bernardo O'Higgins Boulevard flowed before our eyes like a river of light. Even the wan little streetwalkers did not seem as destitute and sad to me as they used to. All at once, the Moneda Palace loomed into view on my side of the taxi like an unwelcome apparition. The last time I saw it, the building was still a burned-out shell covered with ashes in the aftermath of the coup. Restored and once more in use, it now looked like a dream palace at the foot of a French garden.

The grand symbols of the city paraded by us. The Union Club, where the country's prominent *momios* met to pull the strings of traditional politics, the university with its darkened windows, the imposing palace of the National Library, the Paris department store. Beside me, Elena was trying to convince the driver to take us to the El Conquistador Hotel. He insisted on taking us to another hotel, which probably paid him a commission. She was tactful with him, careful not to offend or arouse suspicion, since many Santiago taxi drivers are known to be police informers. I was too dazed to help her persuade him.

As we approached the center of the city, I stopped admiring the material splendor with which the dictatorship sought to cover the blood of tens of thousands killed or disappeared, and ten times that number driven into exile, and instead concentrated on the people in view. They were walking unusually fast, perhaps because curfew was so close. No one spoke, no one looked in any specific direction, no one gesticulated or smiled, no one made the slightest gesture that gave a clue to his state of mind. Wrapped in dark overcoats, each of them seemed to be alone in a strange city. Faces were blank, revealing nothing, not even fear. My mood began to change and I couldn't resist the temptation to get out and lose myself in the crowd. Elena tried to dissuade me, but she couldn't argue with me as vehemently as she would have liked, for fear the driver would overhear. In the grip of uncontrollable emotion, I had the taxi stop and jumped out, slamming the door.

Heedless of the imminent curfew, I walked along Calle Estado, Calle Huérfanos, and through a new zone for pedestrians, closed to traffic, that resembles Calle Florida in Buenos Aires, Via Condotti in Rome, the Place de Beaubourg in Paris, and the Zona Rosa in Mexico City. It was another of the amenities of the dictatorship, yet despite the benches inviting rest and conversation, the gaiety of the lights, and the well-kept flowers in handsome planters, a grim reality showed through. Only on the street corners were there people talking, in low tones inaudible to the prying ears of the dictatorship. There were peddlers and a large number of children begging, but what most caught my attention were the evangelical preachers trying to sell the formula for eternal happiness. Then, all at once, turning into Calle Huérfanos, I saw my first policeman. A *carabinero* was pacing the sidewalk and several more were in a guard booth nearby. I felt an icy hollow in the pit of my stomach and my knees began to buckle. It infuriated me to think that the mere sight of a *carabinero* could so frighten me. However, I quickly realized from their anxious expressions as they watched the passersby that also the policemen were nervous, and this offered some consolation. They had good reason to be. A guard booth on the same spot had been blown up by the underground only a few days before.

17

At the Heart of My Nostalgia

Here were the keys to my past. Nearby had been the old television station and the audiovisual department where I had begun my film career, and the drama school to which I had come from my hometown at the age of seventeen to take the entrance exam that decided my life's work. And it was here too that the Popular Unity demonstrations for Salvador Allende had been held in 1970 and where I had lived my difficult, critical years. I passed the movie theater where I saw the masterpieces for the first time, *Hiroshima, Mon Amour* the most memorable among them. Just then, somebody passed singing Pablo Milanés's song: *I will again walk the streets of what once was bloody Santiago.* I forgot my clandestine situation and returned for a moment to being myself. I had an irrational impulse to identify myself, to shout out my name, to tell the world that it was my right to be home.

I was weeping when I got back to the hotel a step ahead of curfew. The door had just been locked and the concierge had to let me in. Elena had registered for both of us and was in our room hanging up the antenna for the portable radio when I entered. She seemed calm, but the moment I was inside she blew up like a proper wife. It was inconceivable to her that I could have run the risk of walking the streets alone until the last minutes before curfew. I was in no mood for lectures, however, and like a model husband, I slammed the door on my way out. I went to find the Italian crew who were staying at the same hotel.

I knocked on the door of a room two floors below, rehearsing the lengthy password agreed on two months before in Rome with the head of the group. A sleepy voice asked, "Who is it?"

"Gabriel," I answered.

"What else?"

18

"The archangels."

"Saint George and Saint Michael?"

Instead of a note of reassurance entering her voice, it quavered more with each exchange. That seemed strange because she should have been able to recognize my voice after our long talks in Italy. Yet she was dragging out the password even after I had confirmed the names of the archangels.

"Sarco," she said.

That was the surname of the leading character in the film I didn't get to shoot in San Sebastián—*Traveler of the Four Seasons*—and I came back with his first name.

"Nicolás."

Still not enough to satisfy Grazia, a newspaperwoman weathered by many difficult missions.

I then realized that she intended to carry the password game to the bitter end, and I was afraid that this odd wordplay would be overheard in a neighboring room.

"How many feet of film?"

"Stop screwing around and let me in," I growled.

But with the same rigorousness she was to display every moment of the days to follow, she would not open the door until the password was complete.

"Goddammit!" I muttered to myself, thinking not just of Elena but of Ely, too. "They're all alike." And I continued to reply to the interrogation in the manner I most detest in life, that of the housebroken husband. After the last exchange, the door was opened wide and there stood the same youthful and charming Grazia I had known in Italy, who stared at me as if she had seen a ghost and then closed the door in my face. Later she explained, "You looked to me like somebody I had seen before but I wasn't sure who." It was understandable. The Miguel Littín she knew was thoroughly unconventional, dressed any which way, had a beard, and did not wear glasses, while the man who stood at the door was bald, nearsighted, clean-shaven, and dressed like a banker.

"Relax and let me in," I told her. "It's me, Miguel."

Even after examining me closely and finally letting me in, she continued to eye me somewhat dubiously. She had the radio on full volume to drown out our conversation in case of hidden microphones or eavesdroppers. She was quite calm. She had arrived a week earlier with her crew of three and, thanks to the cooperation of her embassy, had obtained the necessary permits and credentials for filming. They had already begun working and had footage of top government officials attending a gala performance of *Madame Butterfly* sponsored by the Italian embassy. General Pinochet had been invited but sent his regrets at the last moment. The fact that the Italian team was there on such an important occasion lent official sanction to our crew's presence in Santiago, and from then on they could operate freely on the streets without arousing suspicion. Also, permission to film inside the Moneda Palace was being processed and Grazia had been assured that there would be no problem.

I was so excited by the news that I wanted to begin filming immediately. If not for the curfew I could have asked Grazia to wake the crew to film a record of the night of my arrival. We made plans to begin shooting early the next morning and agreed that the rest of the group should not be informed of the schedule beforehand and that they must think that it was she and not I who was directing them. Grazia, in turn, would never know that there were two other crews on the same film. We had been making progress between slugs of *grappa*, which she always had with her, when the phone rang. We both jumped. Grazia snatched the receiver, listened briefly, and hung up. It was the reception desk asking that she turn the radio down because there had been a complaint.

A Terrifying Silence Never to Be Forgotten

There had been too much emotion for one day. When I got back to the room I found Elena fast asleep and the light burning on my night table. I undressed without making a sound and got into bed. I had stretched out and closed my eyes when I became aware of the frightening silence of the curfew. There was not a sound in the entire extinguished city. No sound of water running in the pipes, no sound of Elena's breathing, no sound inside my own body.

Nervous and unable to sleep, I got up and stood at the window, looking down at the deserted city, trying to breathe in the open air of the street. I had never seen Santiago so lonely, so sad. Our room was on the fifth floor and faced an alley with high, soot-covered walls, a bit of sky just visible through an ashen mist. I had no sense of being in my own country but felt like a cornered criminal in one of those wintry old films of Marcel Carné.

Twelve years ago, at seven o'clock one morning, an army sergeant had let go a burst of machine-gun fire over my head and ordered me to fall in with a group of prisoners being herded toward the Chile Films building where I worked. The whole city was shuddering with the reverberations of dynamite blasts, gunfire, and low-swooping planes. The sergeant was so confused that he asked me what was going on. "We're neutral," he said. At one point, when we were alone, he asked, "Didn't you direct *El Chacal de Nahualtoro?*"

I told him that I had, and he seemed to forget everything, shots, dynamite blasts, incendiary bombs falling on the Moneda Palace, and asked me to explain how blood was made to appear as though it were flowing out of the wounds of dead people in the movies. He was fascinated by my explanation but snapped back to attention a moment later.

"Don't look behind you," he shouted at us, "or I'll blow your heads off."

One might have thought it was all make-believe were it not for the bodies we had seen in the street a few minutes before, a wounded man bleeding to death on the sidewalk without hope of medical help, gangs of men in civilian clothes clubbing President Allende's supporters to death. We also saw a line of prisoners with their backs against a wall and a squad of soldiers pretending they were going to execute them. But the soldiers who escorted us kept asking us what was happening and repeating, "We're neutral."

The Chile Films building was surrounded by soldiers with machine guns aimed at the entrance. The concierge, wearing a beret with the insignia of the Socialist Party, came out to confront us.

"Aha!" he shouted, pointing at me. "That's Mr. Littín. He's in charge of everything that goes on here."

The sergeant gave him such a violent shove that he fell to the ground. "Drop dead, you piece of shit," he yelled at him.

The sergeant asked me to telephone to find out what was going on. I tried but could not reach anybody. Officers kept entering and leaving. One would give a command and a little later another officer would come in and give a counter-order: we could smoke, we must not smoke; we could sit, we must remain standing. After about half an hour, a young soldier appeared and pointed his rifle at me.

"Hey, Sarge," he said, "there's a lady out there asking about this gentleman."

Ely without a doubt. The sergeant went out to talk to her. Ely had come for my body. In the confusion, a friend told her that I had been executed in front of Chile Films. Meanwhile, the soldiers told us that they had been up since daybreak, that they had had no breakfast, that they were ordered not to accept anything from anybody, that they were cold, that they were hungry. All we could do for them was give them our cigarettes.

The sergeant returned with a lieutenant who began identifying the prisoners to be taken to the stadium. When he came to me, the sergeant cut in before I could answer.

"No, Lieutenant," he said, "this man isn't involved. He just came over to complain that some neighbors were smashing up his car."

The lieutenant looked at me in disgust.

"How can anybody be such a jerk to come around with a complaint like that at a time like this? Tell him to get the hell out of here."

I took off running, convinced that they were going to shoot me in the back on the usual pretext that I was trying to escape. But they didn't. Flags were being hung at various houses on our block as a sign by which the soldiers could identify their sympathizers. Ely and I had already been denounced by a woman who knew about our government connections, my active participation in the Allende presidential campaign, and meetings held in my house when the coup seemed imminent. So we did not go home; for the next month we kept moving from one house to another with the children and the barest essentials, running with death at our heels, until finally the only way out was through the tunnel of exile.

3

Those Who Stayed
Are Also Exiles

At eight o'clock the next morning, I asked Elena to telephone a number only I knew and ask for a person I will call Frankie. When he answered she told him she was calling for Gabriel, who wanted him to come to Room 501 at the El Conquistador. Elena left and I remained in bed. When I heard the knock on the door, less than half an hour later, I pulled the sheet over my head. Frankie had no idea whom he was coming to see since it had been agreed that anybody by the name of Gabriel who phoned him would have been sent by me. In the last week he had been called by three Gabriels who were directing film crews, including Grazia, and he had no reason to suspect that this one was going to be me.

We had been friends since long before the days of the Popular University and he had worked with me on my earliest pictures. More recently, we had gone to various film festivals together and had last met the year before in Mexico. Nevertheless, when I uncovered my head, he did not recognize me until I burst out laughing. This made me a lot more confident about my new look.

I had recruited Frankie for the film at the end of the previous year. He was in charge of receiving the crews, giving them their preliminary instructions, and making all the arrangements necessary for our work without overlapping with Elena's activities. His record was clean. He had gone into voluntary exile in Venezuela after the military coup, with no charges pending against him. Since then he had completed many illegal assignments inside Chile, where he was able to circulate in complete freedom. His popularity among movie people, combined with his engaging personality, quick mind, and boldness, would, I had felt, make him an ideal partner in the adventure. As agreed, he had entered Chile overland from Peru a week before to receive and coordinate the three crews separately, and they were already at work. The French crew was already shooting in the north, from Arica to Valparaíso, in accordance with a detailed schedule its director and I had laid out months before in Paris. The Dutch crew was doing the same in the south. The Italians were to work in Santiago under my direction and were also to be on hold for any unforeseen filming that came up. The three groups had been told to talk to people about Salvador Allende whenever there was no danger of arousing suspicion. We thought that the martyred president was the best point of reference for eliciting an opinion from any Chilean on the country's present situation and future outlook.

Frankie had each crew's itinerary and could get in touch with them at any moment to relay my instructions. He was to act as my driver in cars rented from a different agency every three or four days. We were rarely apart during the course of the filming.

Three with Split Throats Topple a General

We began work at nine in the morning. The Plaza de Armas under the pale sun of the southern autumn was a more moving sight than I had remembered. The Italian crew set up quickly to film the morning routine of retirees reading their newspapers on the wooden steps, old people feeding the pigeons, peddlers, quick-sketch artists, bootblacks, who are thought to be police informers, photographers with their ancient black-sleeved cameras, children flying gaudy balloons around the ice cream carts, people leaving the cathedral. In one corner of the square was the usual group of out-of-work entertainers waiting to be hired for private parties: well-known musicians, magicians, clowns, and transvestites. On this beautiful morning, heavily armed police patrols were posted around the square. Popular songs roared from the loudspeakers atop nearby vans.

I was to learn that the apparent absence of repressive force in the streets was for the benefit of visitors. There were shock squads lurking in the main subway stations at all hours, and water-cannon trucks parked on the side streets ready to put down the outbreaks of protest that were almost a daily occurrence. Surveillance is strictest in the Plaza de Armas, Santiago's nerve center, where the Vicariate of Solidarity has its offices. Headed by Cardinal Silva Henríquez and supported by all who fight for the return of democracy to Chile, it has a moral influence difficult to counteract. The persecuted of all persuasions find refuge and human solidarity in the broad, sunny courtyard of its colonial building. The Vicariate is a reliable source of aid for those in need, particularly political prisoners and their families. Through it, cases of torture are denounced and campaigns are launched on behalf of the *desaparecidos* and against injustice of all kinds.

A few months before my clandestine entry, threats by the dictatorship against the Vicariate had backfired. At the end of February 1985, three opposition militants were kidnapped with such a show of force that there could be no doubt who was responsible. The sociologist José Manuel Parada, an officer of the Vicariate, was taken into custody in front of his children outside their school, with the traffic blocked off for three blocks and the entire sector patrolled by army helicopters. The other two activists were picked up in different parts of the city a few hours apart. One was Manuel Guerrero, head of the Teachers' Union Association of Chile, and the other was Santiago Nattino, a distinguished graphic artist who had not been known as a political militant before. To the nation's horror, the bodies of these three men were found on March 2, 1985, on a lonely road near the international airport, their throats cut and their bodies bearing the signs of torture. General César Mendoza Durán, commander of the police and a member of the junta, made a statement to the press declaring that the triple crime was the result of fighting between communist factions controlled by Moscow. But many believed General Mendoza Durán himself was the perpetrator, and he was forced to resign from the government. Since then the name of Calle Puente, one of the four streets leading to the Plaza de Armas, was erased by an unknown hand and replaced with that of José Manuel Parada, the name by which it is now known.

"I Congratulate You on Being Uruguayan"

The unrest touched off by that savage drama was still in the air the morning that Frankie and I appeared in the Plaza de Armas as two casual strollers. I saw the film crew ready at the location Grazia and I had picked the night before and noted that she saw we were there. Frankie then moved away from me and I took over directing the film according to a method established beforehand with each of the three directors. First, I paced out a route over the cobblestone paths, stopping at various points to indicate to Grazia the length of each shot. Then I retraced my steps to indicate the camera angles. Neither of us was to indicate details that suggested the repressive presence lurking in the streets. This morning was to be devoted strictly to capturing the atmosphere of an ordinary day with emphasis on the behavior of the people who, as I had noticed the night before, seemed much less communicative than they used to be. They walked faster, paying almost no attention to anything around them. Chileans had always gesticulated a great deal, and those in exile still do. But those who conversed in the plaza that morning seemed inhibited and did not use their hands as they talked. I strolled among the groups with a sensitive tape recorder in my pocket, picking up bits of conversation that might prove helpful not only in organizing this stage of the filming but in determining the direction the film would take.

After selecting the points for filming, I sat down in the square to make some notes. The bench I had chosen was covered with hearts and initials carved into its green slats by generations of lovers. Since I did not have my notebook, I wrote on the empty packages of Gitanes cigarettes, of which I had brought a supply from Paris. I did the same throughout the filming and, although that was not the reason that I kept the packages, the notes turned out to be useful as a kind of log for reconstructing the details of my trip for this book.

As I wrote, I noticed that the woman sitting beside me was watching me out of the corner of her eye. She was elderly and was dressed in the old-fashioned style of the lower middle class, with a much-worn hat and a coat with a shabby fur collar. I could not understand what she was doing there, alone and silent, never looking in any particular direction, not even blinking when pigeons fluttered over our heads and pecked at our shoes. She explained to me later that she had gotten chilled at Mass and wanted to sit in the sun for a few minutes before taking the subway home. Pretending to read the paper, I could see that she was studying me from head to toe, probably because my clothes were of a quality not usually seen in the square at that hour. I smiled at her and she asked where I was from. I switched on the tape recorder with an imperceptible pressure on my shirt pocket.

"I'm Uruguayan," I told her.

"Oh," she said. "Congratulations on your good luck."

We both knew that she was alluding to Uruguay's return to the system of democratic elections and she spoke with a tone of nostalgia for her own past. I pretended that my attention was wandering in the hope that she would be more explicit with me about her personal situation. I was not successful, although she did speak openly about the lack of individual freedom and the tragedy of unemployment in Chile. At one point, she indicated the group of out-of-work musicians, clowns, and transvestites, whose numbers were growing.

"Look at those people," she said. "They stand around for days on end waiting for a job to come along. Our country is hungry."

I let her go on talking. When half an hour had passed since I made my first tour of the square, I excused myself and began my second one. Grazia told the cameraman to roll the film without coming in on me for close-ups and to be careful not to draw the attention of the *carabineros* in my direction. Actually, the problem was the other way around. I was the one who couldn't take my eyes off the *carabineros* because they continued to hold a fascination for me that was hard to resist.

Santiago has always had street vendors but I cannot remember ever having seen as many as now. There is hardly a spot anywhere in the business center where they are not standing in long, silent ranks, selling everything imaginable. They are so many and so diverse that their presence alone reveals the social drama. Side by side with a physician who is not permitted to practice, a destitute engineer, a woman with the air of a duchess who is trying to dispose of her wardrobe from

better days at any price, there were orphaned children ped-
dling stolen goods and housewives offering homemade bread.
Most of these once successful professionals have lost everything
but their dignity. Standing behind their wares, they continue
to dress as though they were in their former offices. A taxi
driver, once a wealthy textile merchant, took me on a tour of
half the city that lasted several hours, and at the end he refused
to charge me.

While the cameraman was taking background shots of the
square, I mixed with the people, picking up bits of dialogue
for the soundtrack, taking care that nobody should be com-
promised who might be identifiable on the screen. Grazia
was watching me from another angle and I observed her.
She was following my instructions to begin takes at the highest buildings, then tilt down, gradually panning to the side,
and finish off by filming the *carabineros*. We wanted to catch
the tension in their faces, which became more marked as
activity in the square grew toward midday. It wasn't long,
however, before they noticed the camera's course, realized
they were being watched, and asked to see our permit to
film. I saw Grazia show it to the officer, who seemed satisfied. Relieved, I continued my tour. Later she told me that
this particular *carabinero* had asked her not to photograph
his men, but that he had no answer when she pointed out
that no such exception was stipulated in her permit. She had
invoked her foreign status as an excuse for disobeying an order that did not have the sanction of a higher authority. This
proved that using European crews in Chile did offer the ad-
vantages we had foreseen.

Those Who Stayed Are Also Exiles

The *carabineros* became an obsession with me. I passed very
close to them a number of times looking for a pretext for
conversation. Finally, on impulse, I approached a patrol and

questioned one of the policemen about a colonial building in the city square that had been damaged in the earthquake the previous March and was being rebuilt. The officer who answered never looked at me but kept his eyes constantly on the movement of people in the square. His companion behaved in the same way, but he squinted at me sideways from time to time with growing impatience as he began to note the deliberate foolishness of my questions. Finally he looked me square in the face and with a ferocious scowl barked, "Get moving!"

But I had broken the spell. The anxiety the policemen aroused in me was now transformed into a kind of intoxication, and instead of obeying him, I began giving him a lecture on how the police are supposed to accommodate a harmless foreigner's curiosity. It did not occur to me, however, that my fake Uruguayan accent might not stand up to this difficult test until the *carabinero* got fed up with my lecture and asked for my identification.

Perhaps at no other moment of the entire trip was I jolted by such a shock of sheer panic. I thought of everything: stalling for time, resisting, even bolting, despite the knowledge that I would be caught. I thought of Elena, who could be God knows where at this hour, but the only hope I could summon lay in the cameraman, who would be getting it all down on film, irrefutable proof of my arrest. Also, Frankie had to be somewhere close by and, knowing him as I did, I was certain that he had not let me out of his sight. The easiest thing, of course, would have been to identify myself with my passport, which had withstood the test in numerous airports. I was terrified of being searched, however, because I had committed a fatal error. I had forgotten to remove my true Chilean identity card and a credit card in my own name from the wallet in which I kept the passport. After hesitating a moment, I showed the passport. Not very sure what he was supposed to do, the *carabinero* took a quick glance at the

31

photograph in the document and handed it back to me with a somewhat more amiable expression.

"What is it you wanted to know about that building?" he asked.

I expelled a large lungful of air and answered, "Nothing. I was just being a pain in the ass."

The incident cured me of my *carabinero* complex for the rest of my stay. From then on, I regarded them much as did legal Chileans, or even those of the underground, of whom there are many. On a few occasions, I even went as far as to ask a favor of them, with which they always politely complied. One of these instances, on my last day in Chile, was especially foolhardy. Elena could not conceive how it was possible for anybody to approach the police just to relieve tension, and our working relationship, which was already showing cracks, began to splinter.

At least I can say that I repented my rashness before she or anybody else took me to task. As soon as the *carabinero* returned my passport, I gave Grazia the signal to wind up the shooting. Frankie, who had witnessed the entire episode from the other side of the square as nervously as I, rushed over to my side, but I asked him to pick me up at the hotel after lunch. I wanted to be by myself.

I sat down on a bench to read the newspaper but my eyes ran over the lines without seeing them. What I felt just sitting there on that bright autumn morning was so intense that I couldn't concentrate. All at once, the twelve-o'clock cannon went off, the pigeons scattered in fright, and the notes of Violeta Parra's most moving song, "Gracias a la Vida," floated from the cathedral carillon. It was almost too much to bear. I thought of Violeta, of how often she had gone hungry and homeless in Paris, of her unfaltering dignity. The system had always rejected her, ignored her songs, and mocked her rebelliousness. A president had to die, gun in hand, Chile had to go through the bloodiest martyrdom of its history, and Violeta Parra had to die by her own hand before her country discovered the profound human truth and the beauty of her songs. Even the *carabineros* listened to her devotedly, not having the slightest idea of who she was or what she thought or why she sang. How she would have despised them had she been there on that lovely autumn day.

I went off alone to a restaurant on the heights of the city that Ely and I used to frequent when we were courting. The place was the same, tables out under the elms, a profusion of flowers, but it seemed to have stopped being. There was nobody there. I had to complain to get waited on. Even then, I waited nearly an hour before my order of grilled meat arrived. I was finishing my meal when a couple came in whom I had not seen since Ely and I were regular customers there: Ernesto and Elvira, proprietors of a gloomy little shop a few blocks away that dealt in engravings and medallions of saints, rosaries and reliquaries, funerary decorations. They were an irreverent and fun-loving pair, and we had enjoyed staying late with them on Saturdays in good weather, drinking wine and playing cards. Seeing them enter now, holding hands just as before, I was surprised by their loyalty to the restaurant after all the changes in Chile and I was struck by how much they had aged. It was a mirror in which I suddenly saw an image of my own old age. Had they recognized me they would undoubtedly have stared at me with the same stupefaction, but I was protected by my Uruguayan mask. They were eating at a nearby table and talking in loud tones but without their usual intensity. Occasionally they would look over at me without curiosity, without the slightest inkling that we had once enjoyed each other's company at the same table. It wasn't until that moment that I realized how long and devastating the years of exile had been. Not just for those of us who left—as I had thought until then—but also for the ones who stayed.

33

4

Santiago's Five Cardinal Points

We filmed for five more days in Santiago, which was time enough to test our system. During this period I kept in touch with the French crew in the north and the Dutch crew in the south. Elena's contacts were very efficient and little by little I was conducting the interviews we wanted with underground leaders as well as those few political figures who were working in the open.

I was now resigned to not being me. It was not an easy sacrifice, in view of the fact that there were so many relatives and friends to see—beginning with my parents—and so many moments of my life to relive. But that whole world was off limits to me, at least until the filming was over. Accordingly, I suppressed my innermost feelings and assumed the strange condition of an exile in my own country, the most bitter experience imaginable for me.

I was rarely out on the street unprotected, yet I always felt alone. No matter where I went, the eyes of the resistance were watching over me without my being aware of them. The only time I asked that my protectors be withdrawn was when I had to meet with people whose identities were absolutely confidential and whom I couldn't expose even to my new friends. Later on, by the time Elena had finished helping me get the work started, I was experienced enough to fend for myself and I had no mishaps. The film was made according to plan and none of my colleagues suffered from any carelessness of mine. When we were out of Chile, however, one of the people in charge of the operation told me good-humoredly: "Never in the entire history of the world was security violated as many times and as dangerously."

The main point is that before the end of the first week we were already ahead of schedule in Santiago. We followed a flexible shooting script that allowed for modifications as we went along. In practice, it proved to be the only possible procedure in an unpredictable city that held surprises at every turn and inspired us with cinematic ideas undreamed of before our arrival.

By that time, we had changed hotels three times. The El Conquistador was comfortable and handy, but it was considered a hot spot and we had reason to believe it was one of the most closely watched hotels. There was probably little difference, however, between it and the other five-star hotels, all of which had a constant influx of foreigners who were prime suspects, in principle, of the security forces. As for staying at a second-class hotel, we felt that although its registry would be less rigorously checked by the police, our presence would attract more attention. What seemed safest was to move every three or four days and never go back to a hotel where we had been before. I had a fear of returning to a place where I had already run a risk. This fear went back to September 11, 1973, when the air force bombed the Moneda Palace. The city was in chaos, and I had gone back to the Chile Films offices to see what possibilities there were of resisting the coup. I was able to leave without being bothered but after driving a group of friends who had reason to fear for their lives to Forestal Park in my car, I made the grave mistake of returning to the film building. As I have already related, it was only the miracle of being taken by a soldier who happened to be a film buff that saved my life.

Of all the hotels where we stayed, we had cause for concern in only two. First, the Sheraton. The night we checked in, the telephone rang after I had finally managed to fall asleep. Elena was at a secret meeting that went on longer than anticipated and had to stay overnight because of the curfew, as was to happen several other times. Half-dazed, I answered, not knowing where I was and not remembering quite who. A woman's voice with a Chilean accent was asking for me by my assumed name. I was about to say that I did not know such a person when I was brought fully awake by the implications of such a call at that hour and in that place.

It was the hotel telephone operator with a long-distance call. I realized at once that only Frankie and Elena knew where I was and that it was unlikely that either of them would be calling so late, pretending it was a long-distance call, unless it were a matter of life or death. So I decided to answer. A woman came on with an excited outpouring in English, calling me "darling," "sweetheart," "honey." When I finally managed to convince her that I didn't speak English, she sighed sweetly, muttered "Shit!" and hung up. Attempts to clarify the matter with the operator were useless, except for the discovery that two other guests were registered whose names resembled the one I was using. I was unable to get back to sleep, and as soon as Elena arrived, at around seven o'clock, we moved to another hotel.

The second incident was a scare only in retrospect. We had taken rooms in the dignified old Hotel Carrera, from whose windows it was possible to see the entire Moneda Palace. A few days after we had checked out, a young couple took the room next to the one we had occupied and set up a photographer's tripod on which they mounted a bazooka with a delayed firing mechanism aimed at Pinochet's office. The conception and mechanics of the operation were first-rate and Pinochet was in his office at the right time, but the legs of the tripod gave way with the force of the discharge and the projectile exploded inside the room.

The Five Points

On Friday of our second week, Frankie and I decided to begin our automobile trip to the interior the next day. All that remained to be done in Santiago at that point was the filming in the Moneda Palace and the interviews with figures in open opposition and underground leaders. Arranging the interviews was a complicated business and Elena managed it admirably. The permit for the Moneda Palace had been approved but would not be issued for at least a week, leaving Frankie and me enough time to complete the work in the interior. In view of this, we telephoned instructions to the French crew to return to Santiago as soon as they finished shooting in the north and to the Dutch crew to continue in the south as far as Puerto Montt and to wait there for further word. I would continue working with the Italian crew.

We were going to use that Friday for shots of me in the streets, so that the dictatorship would not be able to claim afterward that I had not directed the film inside Chile. Five characteristic locations in Santiago were selected: the exterior of the Moneda Palace, Forestal Park, the Mapocho bridges, San Cristóbal Hill, and San Francisco Church. We had decided to spend no more than two hours at any one place, a total of ten hours. Grazia had already studied the locations and planned the camera setups days before. I was to arrive fifteen minutes after the crew and, without talking to any of its members, blend into the setting before giving Grazia the prearranged signals for directing the shooting.

The Moneda Palace takes up a square block, its two principal façades facing the Alameda on the Plaza Bulnes side and, on the other, the Plaza de la Constitución, where the presidential offices are. After the building was nearly destroyed during the coup, those offices were moved to the building previously occupied by the United Nations Commission for Trade and Development. Eager for legitimacy, the military government named these temporary headquarters after one of Chile's liberal forefathers, Don Diego Portales, and they remained there until the restoration of the Moneda Palace was completed three years later. In addition to the rebuilding, an underground fortress was constructed in the palace, consisting of armor-plated bunkers with secret passageways, escape hatches, and emergency access to a parking garage under the boulevard. It is said in Santiago, however, that Pinochet's pretensions to historical legitimacy were thwarted by the impossibility of his displaying himself in O'Higgins's presidential sash. This symbol of presidential succession in Chile had been lost in the bombardment of the Moneda Palace. At one point, a crony of the dictatorship tried to substantiate a story that the sash had been saved from the flames by the first officer to occupy the palace but nothing came of the empty claim.

By 9:00 A.M., the Italian crew had filmed the façade on the Alameda site, in front of the monument to the Father of the Country, Bernardo O'Higgins, before which there is a perpetual propane-gas flame, "the flame of freedom." They then moved on to the other façade, where the ceremony of the changing of the guard takes place. It is performed twice a day by the elite *carabineros*, the most spectacular and pompous unit of the palace garrison, before fewer onlookers than at Buckingham Palace, but with the same illusions of grandeur as vigilance on that side of the square is stricter. Accordingly, when the guards saw the Italians preparing to film, they hustled over to ask for the permit that had also been requested on the other side. It was unfailing: once a camera appeared anywhere in the city, *carabineros* turned up asking for a permit.

I arrived at just such a moment. Ugo, the cameraman, an amiable and dedicated young man who was having as much fun as a Japanese tourist with the ongoing adventure of the filming, had set things up so that he could show his papers with one hand while photographing the unsuspecting *carabinero* with the other. Frankie had dropped me four blocks away and was to pick me up fifteen minutes later four blocks farther along. It was a cold, misty morning, typical of Santiago's early autumn, and I was shivering despite my winter overcoat. I had walked the four blocks at a brisk pace among the hurrying crowd in order to keep warm, but I continued for two more blocks to give the team time to finish showing their identification. When I returned, the shots of me walking past the Moneda Palace were taken without a problem. Fifteen minutes later, the crew picked up the gear and headed for the next location. I went to Frankie's car on Calle Riquelme across from Los Héroes subway station and we drove away slowly.

It took less time than we had planned to shoot Forestal Park, but my nostalgia made me linger. The park is a beautiful and characteristic part of Santiago, particularly under a rain of yellow leaves as on this soft autumn morning. The School of Fine Arts is there. I had presented my first theater piece on its steps a few months after arriving from my hometown. Years later, as a budding film director, I would cross the park almost daily. The soft glow of evening light on the park's foliage is entwined forever with memories of my first films. A short sequence of me strolling among the trees shedding their leaves, accompanied by a whisper of rain, took care of the shoot. From the park I kept on walking as far as the business center, where Frankie was waiting.

The weather had turned clear and cold and, for the first

time since my arrival, the cordillera appeared sharply outlined in the distance. Santiago is in a valley between mountains and the cordillera is usually seen through a haze of pollution. When we arrived at Calle Estado almost an hour before noon, the street was crowded and people were already going into movie theaters for the first show of the day. The Rex, nearby, was playing Milos Forman's *Amadeus*, which I was dying to see, but this time I exercised some restraint and met Frankie as planned.

And Around the Corner, My Mother-in-law!

I had recognized many acquaintances, journalists and artists, even some politicians, as they passed us in the streets during the filming, yet not one of them looked at me with the slightest sign of recognition. Late on Friday, however, something happened that was bound to happen, sooner or later. I saw a distinguished-looking woman approaching me, dressed in a two-piece cream-colored twill dress, without an overcoat. I did not realize who it was until she was less than ten feet away from me. It was my mother-in-law, Leo. Not only had we seen each other only six months earlier in Spain, but she knew me so well that it would have been impossible for her not to recognize me at such close quarters. I thought of turning around but remembered I had been warned to control that impulse, which can often bring the danger of being recognized from behind. I trusted my mother-in-law enough not to be alarmed if she did recognize me, but she was not alone. Aunt Mina, her sister, who also knew me, was with her and they were talking in low tones, almost whispering. What I feared most was a sudden reaction. I wouldn't have been surprised if they had exclaimed, right there on the street: "Miguel, my boy! You got in! How wonderful!" or something of the kind. Besides, it was dangerous for them to know that I was underground in Chile.

Because there was nothing else to be done, I kept walking and stared at Leo with the most intense concentration possible in order to check her immediately should she recognize me. She barely raised her eyes as she went by, met my fixed, terrified gaze without stopping her conversation with Aunt Mina, and looked straight at me without seeing me. We passed so close that I could smell her perfume and see her beautiful, gentle eyes. I even heard her whispered voice saying clearly, "Children are more of a problem when they are grown-up." Then she walked on.

I mentioned the encounter to her not long ago on the phone from Madrid and she was astonished that she had not known. Shaken by the incident, I looked for a place to sit and collect myself. I went into a little movie theater that was showing *Happiness Island*, an all but pornographic Italian film. For ten minutes I watched slim men and beautiful women leaping into the sea on a dazzling day somewhere in Paradise. I didn't even try to concentrate, I let the darkness help me regain my composure. I had not realized until then how routine and placid the previous days had been. At 11:45, Frankie picked me up on the corner of Calle Estado and the Alameda and took me to the next location, the Mapocho bridges.

The Mapocho River runs through the city over a cobblestone bed crossed by handsome bridges whose magnificent iron structures are earthquakeproof. In times of drought, as it was then, the flow of the river is reduced to a stagnant thread of liquid clay. Dilapidated shacks are perched on its banks. In the rainy season the swift currents off the cordillera flood the shores and the shacks float like small boats adrift on a sea of mud. In the months following the military coup, the Mapocho River became notorious for the mutilated corpses carried by its waters after night attacks by army patrols in the slum barrios, the famous *poblaciones*. Now the starving mobs fight the dogs and vultures for leftovers thrown into the Mapocho from the popular markets. This tragedy is the other face of the "Chilean miracle," sponsored by the military junta under the tutelage of the Chicago School of economists.

Not only was Chile a modest country until the end of Allende's regime but even its conservative bourgeoisie considered austerity a national virtue. To give an immediate and impressive appearance of prosperity, the military junta denationalized everything that Allende had nationalized, selling off almost anything of value to private capital and multinational corporations. The result was an explosion of flashy luxury goods and decorative public works that created an illusion of spectacular wealth and economic stability.

Within a five-year period more goods were imported than in the previous two hundred years, using dollar credits guaranteed by the National Bank with money obtained from the denationalizations. The United States, in complicity with international credit agencies, did the rest. But when the time came to pay up, the illusions fell away: the economic fantasies of six years vanished in one. Chile's external indebtedness increased to $23 billion, almost six times the debt of the Allende administration. A walk through the popular markets on the banks of the Mapocho River gives a grim account of the social effect of $19 billion wasted. The economic miracle made a few of the rich much richer and the rest of Chilean society much poorer.

The Bridge That Has Seen Everything

In the midst of the carnival of life and death, the Recoleta Bridge is an indiscriminate lover, serving markets and cemetery alike. During the day, funerals push their way through the crowds. At night, when there is no curfew, Recoleta is the only road to the tango clubs, where the best dancers are gravediggers by day. What most caught my attention that

Friday, after so many years away, was the number of young lovers strolling along the terraces that overlook the river. Arms around each other's waists, they seemed to be loving one another slowly, heedless of the time slipping away pitilessly. Only in Paris had I seen so much loving in the streets, and that was years ago. I remembered Santiago as a city of private sentiments. Now I found myself witness to a sight that had gradually died out in Paris and was, I had thought, gone from the world. I thought of something I had heard not long before in Madrid: "Love blossoms in times of the plague."

The Chileans of the dark suits and umbrellas, the women hanging on the latest fashions and novelties from Europe, the babies in their prams dressed up like rabbits—these had all been swept away by the refreshing wind of the Beatles. That was before the time of Popular Unity. Then there was a definite trend in fashion toward overlapping of the sexes. Women cut their hair nearly down to the scalp and adopted men's tight-seated, wide-legged trousers, while the men let their hair grow long. This in turn was all swept aside by the fanatic prudery of the dictatorship. An entire generation had to cut their hair if they didn't want it hacked off with bayonets by army patrols, as often happened in the early days of the coup.

I did not realize until that day at the Mapocho bridges how much the young had changed. The city was taken over by the generation that followed mine. Children who were ten years old when I left, and scarcely capable of appreciating the magnitude of the catastrophe, were now twenty-two. The elementary school children of Salvador Allende's time are now the resistance commanders. This was an exciting discovery but also an upsetting one for me: now, for the first time, I had to question whether this harvesting of my nostalgia was worth the trouble.

The doubt gave me fresh drive. To complete the day's program, I made a quick swing by San Cristóbal Hill and then over to San Francisco Church, whose stones were turning to gold in the afternoon sunlight. Then I asked Frankie to get my suitcase from the hotel and to pick me up in three hours outside the Rex, where I went to see *Amadeus*. I also asked him to tell Elena that he and I were going to disappear for three days. That was all. This violated the established norm that Elena should at all times know my whereabouts, but I couldn't help it. Frankie and I were off on the eleven-o'clock train that night to Concepción for as long as necessary.

5

A Man in Flames
Before the Cathedral

We had decided to take this trip on the spur of the moment, yet our reasoning was sound. The train seemed to me the best way of traveling inside Chile since there were none of the identity checks that took place at airports and on highways and because the nights, which were dead time under the curfew, could be used fruitfully. Frankie was not so convinced of the safety of trains because he knew that they were the most closely watched means of transportation. I argued that they were safer precisely for that reason. It would never occur to a policeman that a clandestine person would get on a train under surveillance. Frankie thought the police knew that underground people travel by train because they think the more closely watched the conveyance, the safer it is. He also believed that a wealthy advertising man with wide experience and important business dealings in Europe would be likely to use the fine railways there but not the poor ones in Chile's interior. However, he was finally won over by my argument that the plane to Concepción is not the surest way of keeping to a schedule, since it is impossible to know when the fog will permit landing. To be honest, I would have preferred the train anyway because of my incurable fear of flying.

We took the 11:00 P.M. train from the central station, whose iron structure has the same ineffable beauty as the Eiffel Tower, and installed ourselves in a clean and comfortable compartment of the pullman car. I was starving. I had had two chocolate bars as breakfast in the movie theater just at the moment young Mozart was executing acrobatic leaps before the emperor of Austria. I had eaten nothing since. The conductor informed us that there was a dining car but that regulations required that it be sealed off from the pullman. He suggested that we could go to the dining car before the train pulled out, eat whatever we wanted, and return to our car at the Rancagua stop an hour later. We ran as fast as we could because curfew had already sounded and the conductors were hustling us along, shouting, "Hurry, gentlemen, hurry, we are breaking the law." At the Rancagua station, however, the guards, sleepy and half frozen, didn't give a damn about such an unavoidable and tolerable breach of martial law.

It was an empty and icy station, deserted, wrapped in a ghostly fog. It looked like train stations in films about deportations in Nazi Germany. Suddenly, as the conductors were urging us on, a waiter from the dining car appeared in his classic white coat, running like a hare, a plate of rice with a fried egg on top balanced on the palm of his hand. He raced ahead of us some fifty yards at breakneck speed, the plate still magically balanced. He handed it in through the window of the last car and was clambering back into the diner before we reached our pullman.

We covered the 300 miles to Concepción in total silence. It was as though the curfew were compulsory not only for the passengers of that somnambulant train but for all the creatures of nature. From time to time I looked out of the window but all I could make out through the fog were empty stations, empty fields, the vast empty night of the uninhabited countryside. The only proof of man's existence on earth was the endless barbed-wire fence along the right of way with nothing beyond it, no people, no flowers, no animals . . . nothing. I thought of Pablo Neruda: *Bread, rice, apples, everywhere; in Chile, wire, wire, wire.* At seven o'clock in the morning, with plenty of territory still ahead before the barbed wire came to an end, we arrived in Concepción.

Before deciding what to do next, we thought it would be a good idea to see where we could get a shave, although I would have taken advantage of any pretext to let my beard grow. Unfortunately, we would look like desperados to the *carabineros* in that city known to all Chileans as the cradle of the country's great social struggles. There the student movement of the seventies was born, there Salvador Allende received the decisive support he needed for his election, and there President Gabriel González Videla launched the brutal repressions of 1946 before he set up the Pisagua concentration camp. As a young officer, Augusto Pinochet was trained at that infamous camp in the arts of terror and death.

Eternal Flowers in Plaza Sebastián Acevedo

As we drove toward the center of the city, through the dense and frigid mist we could see the lone cross in the atrium of the cathedral and the perpetual bouquet of flowers brought by anonymous friends. Sebastián Acevedo, a coal miner, had set himself on fire on that spot two years before, after fruitless efforts to find somebody to intercede for him at the National Center for Information to stop the torture of his twenty-two-year-old son and twenty-year-old daughter who had been arrested for illegal possession of arms.

Sebastián Acevedo did not plead, but he gave warning. The archbishop was away on a trip, so he spoke to officers of the archbishopric, to reporters of the leading newspapers, to the heads of political parties, to leaders of business and industry, to anyone who would listen, even to government officials, saying the same thing to everyone: "If you don't do something to stop the torture of my children, I will soak myself with gasoline and set myself on fire in the atrium of the cathedral." Some did not believe him. Others did not know what to do. Sebastián Acevedo stood in the atrium on the appointed day, emptied a pail full of gasoline over his body, and warned the crowd gathered in the street that if anyone crossed the yellow line he would immediately set himself on fire. A *carabinero*, in an effort to stop the immolation, stepped over the line, and Sebastián Acevedo became a human bonfire.

He lived for seven hours, lucid and suffering no pain. The public outcry was so great that the police were obliged to allow his daughter to visit him in the hospital before he died. But the doctors did not want her to see him in such a horrible condition and would allow her to talk to him only on an intercom. "How do I know you are Candelaria?" Sebastián Acevedo asked when he heard her voice. She told him the pet name he used to call her when she was little. The brother and sister were released from the torture chambers, as the martyred father had demanded in giving his life for theirs, and they were placed under the jurisdiction of the regular courts. Since that time, the people of Concepción have had a secret name for the place of sacrifice: Plaza Sebastián Acevedo.

It's Not So Easy to Get a Shave in Concepción

To appear in that historic stronghold at seven in the morning, disguised as a foreign businessman, but unshaven, wasn't the risk. Everyone knows that, in their attaché cases, executives today carry, together with their miniaturized dictation machines for recording their ideas, a battery-powered razor to use on the plane or train, or in the car before appearing at business meetings. Nevertheless, it probably wasn't a huge risk to look for someone who could give me a decent shave at seven o'clock on a Saturday morning. First I tried at the only barbershop near the Plaza de Armas open at that hour. A sign on the door said: UNISEX. A young woman of about twenty was sweeping the place and a young man of more or less the same age was arranging bottles on a shelf.

"I'd like a shave," I said.

"We don't do that here," the man answered.

"Where do they?"

"Try farther up. There are lots of barbershops."

I walked one block to where Frankie had stopped to rent a car and found him with two *carabineros*, identifying himself. They asked me for my papers also. There was no problem. Quite the contrary: while Frankie was arranging for the car, one of them walked me to another barbershop that was just opening, where he said good-bye and shook hands with me.

It had the same sign on the door: UNISEX. As in the first shop, a woman of about thirty-five and a young man were there. The man asked what I wanted. I said I would like a shave and the two of them looked at me in surprise.

"No, sir, we don't have that service here," he said.

"We're unisex," said the girl.

"Fine," I said to them, "but unisex as you may be, if a person needs a shave you can still give him one, can't you?"

"No, sir," the man answered, "not here."

With that they turned their backs on me. I kept walking the deserted streets through the oppressive mist. It was surprising how many unisex barbershops there were in Concepción. So was the uniformity of their policy: nobody would give me a shave. I was lost in the fog when a boy who was passing in the street asked me, "Are you looking for something, mister?"

"Yes," I told him, "a barbershop that isn't unisex but just for men, like the ones there used to be."

He guided me to a barbershop with the traditional red-and-white-spiral cylinder at the entrance and old-fashioned swivel chairs. Two old barbers wearing dirty aprons were taking care of the only customer. One was cutting his hair and the other brushing off what fell on his face and shoulders. The place smelled of liniment, mentholated alcohol, and old-time drugstore. Not until then did I realize that this odor was what I missed in the other shops, the odor of my boyhood days.

"I'd like a shave," I said.

Both barbers and the customer looked at me in surprise. The old man with the brush asked me the question that was undoubtedly in the minds of all three: "Where are you from?"

Automatically, I answered, "Chile," and hastening to correct myself, added, "but I'm Uruguayan."

Nobody noticed that the correction was worse than the error but I realized from their reaction that the word *rasurar*, which I had used for the verb "to shave," had not been used in Chile for some time; it had been supplanted by the more common *afeitar*. The young people in the unisex barbershop also did not understand my choice of outdated words. In this place, on the contrary, everybody brightened up at the arrival of a person who spoke as they had in their better days, and the barber who was free sat me in his chair, wrapped a sheet around my neck in a familiar way, and brought out an old nicked razor. He was at least seventy years old and looked as if none of them had been easy. Tall and flabby, with very white hair, his own face was covered with three days of stubble.

"Do you want your shave with hot water or cold?" he asked.

He was barely able to hold the razor in his shaky hand.

"Hot water, of course."

"In that case, we're in trouble, sir," he said, "because there's no hot water here, just plain cold."

I went back to the first unisex barbershop, and when I made the same request using *afeitar* instead of *rasurar*, I was waited on immediately, but on condition that I have my hair cut as well. When I agreed, the young pair dropped their indifference and initiated a prolonged ritual. First, she wrapped a towel around my neck and gave me a shampoo in cold water—no hot water there, either. Then she asked if I wanted a face pack with formula number three, four, or five. After that they suggested a treatment for falling hair. I went along with everything until, while drying my face, she suddenly stopped and said, as if to herself, "How strange!"

I opened my eyes with a start and asked, "What?"

She was more flustered than I but she had to answer.

"Your eyebrows are plucked," she said.

Displeased by her discovery, I decided to indulge in the ugliest joke I could make. Casting her a languid glance, I said, "And why not? Are you prejudiced against gays?"

She blushed to the roots of her hair and shook her head. Then the barber took over and, despite my detailed instructions, cut my hair shorter than he should have, combed it differently, and ended up changing me back to Miguel Littín. It was logical, because the Paris makeup expert had purposely gone against the natural tendency of my hair. All the Concepción barber did was put things back in their normal place. It would be easy enough to comb it back to the style of my other self, which was, in fact, what I did. Yet it took considerable willpower to resist my longing to be myself again in this remote, foggy city where nobody would recognize me anyway. After the haircut, the young woman took me into the rear of the shop and furtively, as though about to engage in an indecent act, plugged in a razor in front of a mirror and handed it to me to use. No hot water was necessary, fortunately.

A Love Paradise in Hell

Frankie had arranged the car rental. Our breakfast was a cup of cold coffee at a soda fountain that also had no hot water. Then we set out for the Lota and Schwager coal mines via the great bridge over Chile's mightiest river, the Bío-Bío, whose somnolent, metallic waters were barely visible through the fog. A detailed description of the mines and the life of the miners, written in the last century by a Chilean, Baldomero Lillo, is just as fitting today. Being in the mining region is like being in the Wales of a hundred years ago, as much for the soot-impregnated mist as for working conditions that still predate the Industrial Revolution.

We had to pass through three checkpoints before getting there. The first was the most difficult, as we knew it would be. Consequently, when the guards asked us what we would be doing at Lota and Schwager, we pulled out all the stops. I surprised even myself with the eloquence of my reply. I said that we were there to see with our own eyes the park famed as the most beautiful in America for its gigantic old araucaria trees and the extraordinary spectacle of its many statues surrounded by peacocks of ill omen and swans with black throats. I explained our plan to use the park as the background for a promotional film that would spread throughout the world the name of Araucaria, a new perfume named in tribute to this idyllic spot.

Not a Chilean policeman alive could have resisted an explanation that long, especially when it included exorbitant praise of his country's natural beauty. They welcomed us and must have notified the next checkpoint of our arrival, since we were not asked to show our papers. Our luggage and the car, however, were examined. They were interested only in the super-8 camera—although it was not a professional model—because a permit is required for filming in the mines. We explained that we were going only as far as the park with the statues and swans, at the top of the mountain, and I tried to conclude with a show of snobbish disdain.

"We aren't interested in seeing the poor," I told them.

Examining each article closely, one of the *carabineros* remarked, without looking at me, "Everybody around here is poor."

They were satisfied with the inspection. Half an hour later, we passed through the third checkpoint at the end of a steep and narrow ledge and arrived at the park. It was a bizarre place built by Don Matías Cousiño, a famous winegrower, for the woman he loved. He collected marvelous trees from all corners of Chile for her pleasure; he brought in mythological animals, statues of improbable gods representing spiritual states: joy, sadness, nostalgia, love. There was a fairy-tale palace at the rear, from whose terraces one could see across the Pacific to the other side of the world.

We spent the entire morning there filming in super-8 the places that the crew would shoot after the necessary permission was obtained. We had no sooner taken the first shots when a guard came over to tell us that any kind of filming was forbidden. We repeated the story of the promotional film to be shown all over the world, but he stuck to his orders. He offered to accompany us to the mines below so that we could ask his superiors for permission.

"We won't film any more now," I told him, "but come along with us if you like, so you can be sure."

He agreed and we toured the park again with him. He was a young man with a sad face. Frankie kept the conversation going but I preferred not to talk in my bad Uruguayan accent any more than absolutely necessary. At one point, when the guard wanted to smoke, we gave him all our cigarettes. He left us alone then and we went on filming whatever we thought useful. Not only above in the park, but below, outside the mines. We established the setups that interested me most, the angles, lenses, distances, the vast scope of the great park, and then the squalor below, where the lives of the miners and fishermen overlap. It is a Manichean place, real yet almost unimaginable.

The Bar Where the Seagulls Go to Sleep

It was late in the afternoon when we came down. The launches that make the daily trip to nearby Santa María Island were setting out over a horrendous sea of enormous black waves, carrying entire families loaded down with old tools and private possessions and animals to eat. The coal miners are in deep tunnels that run beneath the ocean floor; here, thousands of miners work under agonizing conditions. Outside, hundreds of men and women together with their children scratch like moles at the earth around the tunnel entrances, tearing at the tailings from the mine with their nails. In the park above, the air, oxygenated by the trees, is clear and pure. Below, miners breathe in the cloud of coal dust, which burns as it enters and settles in the lungs. Seen from above, the sea is of unimaginable beauty. Below, it is turbid and roaring.

This was one of Salvador Allende's strongholds. The "coal march," as it was called, took place here in 1958. The miners crossed the bridge over the Bío-Bío as a dark, silent mob that took the city of Concepción with flags and placards raised in their arms, and with a determination to fight that stunned the government. The incident was recorded by Sergio Bravo in his film *Banderas del Pueblo* (Flags of the People), one of the most moving Chilean documentaries ever made. Allende was in that march, and I believe it was there that he received firm proof of the people's support. Later, on one of his first trips as president, he went to talk and listen to the miners in the square of Lota.

I was in his entourage. I was struck to hear a man like him, so proud of his youthful vitality at sixty, saying something that day that came from his guts: "I am no longer young. I'm practically an old man now." The miners, withered, leaden-faced, impenetrable, hardened by years of unkept promises, opened themselves to him and gave themselves as a group to his cause. One of the first decisions he made as president was to nationalize the mines as he had promised that afternoon at Lota and Schwager. One of Pinochet's first acts was to return the mines to private ownership, as he did with just about everything else: cemeteries, railroads, ports, even the collection of garbage.

At 4:00 P.M., when the filming at the mines was finished without any interference by soldiers or civil authorities, we returned to Concepción by way of Talcahuano, making our way through the densely packed mass of miners who, on their way home in the fog, dragged carts loaded with chunks of coal retrieved from the mine. Diminutive, ghostly men and tiny, strong women carrying huge bags of coal, creatures out of a nightmare, suddenly appearing out of the twilight, barely visible in the headlights.

Talcahuano, headquarters of the naval school for petty officers, is Chile's principal military port and most active shipyard. The air there is tainted with the stench of the fish-meal factories, the tar from the shipyards, and the putrefaction of the sea. In the days following the coup it had the sad privilege of being the point of departure for prisoners bound for the hell of Dawson Island. On the streets the young cadets in their spotless uniforms mingle with the horde of ragged miners.

Contrary to what we had expected, the army did not check travelers. Most of the houses were dark and the few lights in the windows seemed to come from oil lamps. We had not eaten since the breakfast of cold coffee so the unexpected sight of a brightly lit restaurant was like an apparition, and even more so when we found it filled with seagulls that entered over the cliffs from the sea. I had never seen so many and had never seen them rising out of the darkness, swooping over the impassive customers, flying as though blind, stunned, crashing about like a band of drunken pirates boarding a ship. We breakfasted at suppertime on antediluvian Chilean shellfish that taste of deep, icy waters, and then returned to Concepción. The car-rental office had been closed and we lost nearly four hours trying to find somebody who would let us return the car. The train to Santiago was already moving when we slipped on board.

6

Two of the Dead Who
Never Die:
Allende and Neruda

The *poblaciones*, vast labyrinths of poverty in Chile's major cities, are in a sense liberated territories—like the casbah of Arab cities—whose inhabitants have created a culture of subversion. The police and the army hesitate before entering these beehives, where even an elephant could be made to disappear without a trace. The slums have always been a headache for the government. Even during the democratic regimes of Chile, their historic status turned the *poblaciones* into partisan centers of political unrest. It was our task to capture in cinema-verité style what the poor think about the dictatorship and the degree to which Salvador Allende's memory lives among them.

We were surprised that the names of the leading resistance figures in exile mean little to the new generation now fighting the dictatorship. They are considered heroes of a glorious past that doesn't have much to do with the present. Although it may sound like a contradiction, this could be the military regime's gravest failure. At the beginning of his administration, General Pinochet declared that he would remain in power until the last vestige of the democratic system had been erased from the memory of the new generation. It didn't occur to him that his own regime might be wiped out someday instead. Not long ago, exasperated by the courage of boys who would fight off riot police with nothing more than stones and who plot to reestablish a system they have never known firsthand, General Pinochet declared that the younger generation is fighting against him only because it has no conception of what democracy in Chile was like.

The past is kept alive in the name of Salvador Allende. The cult that has grown around his memory has already reached the proportion of legend in the *poblaciones*. We particularly wanted to explore the living conditions of the people, their reaction to the dictatorship, and their methods of resistance. The answers to our questions were always spontaneous and frank, and always tied to the memory of Allende. The many individual testimonials all sounded the same: "I always voted for him, never for his opponent." Allende ran for office so many times that he used to say his epitaph would read: *Here lies Salvador Allende, future president of Chile.* In his long parliamentary career, he had been a candidate in most of the provinces from the Peruvian border to Patagonia. Although he had been a deputy and a senator many times over, it took four hard campaigns before he finally won the presidency. As a consequence, he not only knew every inch of the country, its people, its customs, its disappointments, and its dreams, but was himself known in the flesh by the entire population. Unlike many politicians who are known only through the newspapers, television, or radio, Allende conducted his campaign in the home, in warm, direct contact with the people, like a family doctor, which is what he was. His almost animal-like instinct for the craft of politics provoked contradictory feelings even among his supporters. One day, when he was already president, a man paraded before him in a demonstration carrying a sign that bore the unusual message: *This is a shitty government, but it's my government.* Allende stood up, applauded, and came down to shake his hand.

In our long trips around the country we did not come upon a place where he had not left something of himself. There was always a person whose hand he had shaken, whose child he had been godfather to, whom he had cured of a stubborn cough with a tea he prepared from the leaves of a plant in his own yard. Or there would be somebody for whom he had gotten a job or against whom he had won a chess game. Anything he touched was preserved as a relic. When least expected, we would be shown a chair in better condition than others and would be told: "He once sat here." Or people would show us some small figurine and say, "He gave us this." A young woman who already had one child and was pregnant with another, said to us, "I always show my little boy who the president was, even though I barely knew him myself because I was only nine years old when he went." We asked what she remembered about him and she answered: "I was with my father and saw him talking on a balcony and waving a white handkerchief." In one house where there was an image of the Carmelite Virgin we asked its owner whether she had been an *allendista.* "Not had been, *am,*" she responded quickly. She removed the image of the Virgin, revealing a photograph of Allende behind it.

Small busts of the former president were sold in the popular markets during his administration. Now floral offerings and votive lamps are placed before these relics in the homes. His memory is kept alive in the old people who voted four times for him, in those who voted three times, in those who elected him, and in the children who know him only through stories. Several women we interviewed told us the same thing: "Salvador Allende was the only president who ever spoke of women's rights." They rarely used his name, calling him "the president." It was as though he were still the president—as though he had been the only one—and they were only waiting for him to return. More than his image, however, his humanistic philosophy is deeply ingrained in the memory of the *poblaciones*. "It's not a roof over our heads or food that we're worrying about. Let them give us back our dignity," the poor say. "All we want is what they took from us: a say in our lives."

Two of the Dead Who Live

The Allende cult is most evident in Valparaíso, the bustling port city where he was born, grew up, and trained for a life in politics. There he read his first theoretical works in the home of an anarchist shoemaker and was smitten by his lifelong passion for chess. His grandfather Ramon Allende founded the first secular school in Chile and established its first Masonic lodge, in which Salvador Allende attained the highest rank of grand master. His earliest political activity came during the "twelve socialist days," organized by the legendary Marmaduque Grove, whose brother married Allende's sister.

It is strange that the dictatorship should have buried Allende in Valparaíso, the place he himself would undoubtedly have chosen. With no announcement or ceremony he was taken there on the night of September 11, 1973, accompanied only by his wife, Hortensia Bussi, and his sister, Laura, in an antiquated propeller plane of the air force, with the icy southern wind blowing in through its cracks. A former member of the military junta's intelligence service who entered the Moneda Palace with the first attackers told a U.S. newspaperman, Thomas Hauser, that he had seen the president's body "with the head open and the remains of the brain spattered on the floor and the walls." That may explain why, when Allende's widow asked to see his face in the coffin, they refused to expose it and allowed her to see only a form covered by a sheet. He was buried in the mausoleum of Marmaduque Grove's family in the Santa Inés cemetery with no other offering than the bouquet of flowers placed there by his widow as she said: "Salvador Allende, president of Chile, is buried here." The dictatorship hoped they could move Allende out of the reach of popular veneration, but it was not possible. Although the government went so far as to spread a rumor that the body had been moved, pilgrims continue to arrive daily and gifts of flowers are left anonymously on the gravestone.

The cult of Pablo Neruda also thrives among the new generation, and the poet's former seaside home at Isla Negra has become its shrine. Despite its name, this legendary place is neither an island nor black, but a fishing village with yellow dirt paths running between giant pine trees and a wild green sea, located twenty-five miles south of Valparaíso near the San Antonio highway. Pablo Neruda's house there is a mecca for lovers from the world over. Frankie and I had gone ahead to set up a shooting schedule while the Italian crew was finishing up the last shots in Valparaíso. The *carabinero* on duty showed us where the bridge was, and the inn, and the other places celebrated by the poet in his verses, but he warned me that it was forbidden to visit the house.

While waiting at the inn for the others to arrive, we could appreciate how the poet had been the soul of Isla Negra. Whenever he was there, the place would be overrun by young people carrying his *Twenty Love Poems* as their only guidebook. All they wanted was to see him for a moment or, perhaps, to ask for an autograph. For most, it was enough to take away a memory of the place. In those days the inn was a gay and noisy place where Neruda would appear from time to time in one of his gaudy ponchos and Andean cap, bulky and as slow-moving as the pope. He would come there to use the telephone—he had had his own removed to avoid interruptions—or to discuss with Doña Elena, the proprietress, how to prepare a dish for friends the same night at his house. Neruda was an expert in culinary delights and could cook like a professional himself. He had refined the art of good eating to such a degree that he fussed over even the smallest details of the table setting and was quite capable of changing cloth, dishes, or silverware until they were in harmony with the food being served. Twelve years later, all of that had been swept away by a desolate wind. Doña Elena, overwhelmed by her painful memories, had left for Santiago and the inn was near collapse. One scrap of poetry remained: since the last earthquake, tremors continued to be felt at Isla Negra every ten or fifteen minutes of every day and through the night.

The Earth Trembles at Isla Negra

We found Neruda's house in the shade of its sentinel pines, surrounded by the fence several feet high with which the poet had protected his private life. Flowers had sprung from the wood. A sign warned that the house had been sealed by the police and that it was forbidden to enter or take photographs. The *carabinero* who passed on his round at regular intervals was even more blunt: "Everything is forbidden here." Aware of this beforehand, the Italian cameraman had brought heavy, impressive equipment to be surrendered at the guard post, while another, portable outfit was hidden in his clothes. Also, our group traveled in three cars so that the rolls of exposed film could be taken to Santiago as soon as they were shot. Only the material in the camera would be lost if we were caught. Should this happen, the crew would pretend not to know us and Frankie and I would become innocent tourists.

The doors of the house were locked from the inside, the windows had been covered with white curtains, and the flag that signaled Neruda's presence was absent from the pole. Amid so much sadness, the garden flourished at the hands of anonymous caretakers. Neruda's widow, Matilde, who had died shortly before our visit, removed the furniture after the coup, as well as the books and the collections of everything human and divine that Neruda had gathered in his itinerant life. His houses in various parts of the world were distinguished not by their simplicity but by their extravagance. His passion for capturing nature was not restricted to his masterful poetry. He amassed collections of twisted seashells, figureheads from ships, nightmarish moths and butterflies, strange glasses and goblets. In one of his houses, visitors might come upon a horse standing in the middle of an office, stuffed, but looking as if it were alive. Neruda would rearrange the architecture of his houses at whim. One remarkable renovation cut the living room off from the dining room, and it took a walk through the patio to get from one room to the other, with umbrellas graciously provided during the rainy season. Neruda's Venezuelan friends who associated bad taste with bad luck told him that his collections would bring him harm. Greatly amused, he would reply that poetry is the antidote to bad luck and his frightful collections had proved this beyond a doubt.

His principal residence was his house on Calle Marqués de la Plata in Santiago, where he died a few days after the coup, of chronic leukemia exacerbated by grief. This house was sacked by soldiers who threw his books onto a bonfire in the garden. With his Nobel Prize money, Neruda bought what had been the stable of a castle in Normandy, remodeled as a dwelling and standing at the edge of a pond with lotus flowers. It had tall ceilings like the vaults of a church, and the light entering through the stained-glass windows tinted the poet with radiant colors as he sat in bed receiving his friends. He did not live to enjoy it for even a year.

His Isla Negra house is the one Neruda's readers associate

with his poetry. A new generation of admirers, who could not have been more than eight years old when the poet was alive, continues to gather there. They come from all over the world to draw hearts entwined with initials and to write messages of love on the fence that blocks the entrance. Most of them are variations on the same theme: *Juan and Rosa love each other through Pablo. Thank you, Pablo, for teaching us love. We want to love as much as you loved.* But there are others that the *carabineros* can't prevent or erase, such as *Generals: Love never dies. Allende and Neruda live. One minute of darkness will not make us blind.* They are written in the most unexpected spots, and the entire fence gives the impression that, for lack of space, several generations of inscriptions have been superimposed. If anybody had the patience to do it, the complete poems of Pablo Neruda could be reconstructed from the scattered verses written from memory on the fence boards by lovers. Those words seemed to take on life every ten or fifteen minutes with the profound tremors that shook the earth. The fence tried to push away from the earth, wood creaked at the joints, there was a tinkling of glassware and metal as on a yacht adrift, and one had the impression that the whole world was trembling with all the love sown in the garden of that house.

At the moment of truth, our precautions had been unnecessary. Our camera was not confiscated and no one bothered us simply because the *carabineros* had gone to lunch. We filmed everything we had planned and, thanks to Ugo, much more. He went berserk with the effect of the tremors in the sea and walked up to his waist into the waves that broke against the rocks with a prehistoric roar. He was risking his life: even without the earthquakes, the tremendous undertow could have dragged him down. But it was impossible to hold him back. Ugo filmed without stopping, without being directed, glued to the viewfinder. Anybody who knows the movie profession from inside knows that it is impossible to control or direct a cameraman possessed.

"Grazia Went to Heaven"

As planned, every roll of film was rushed to Santiago as soon as it was exposed so that Grazia could take the rolls of film with her to Italy all at once. Her departure date had not been chosen casually. For the last week we had been studying the best way to get the material already filmed out of Chile since the underground channels provided in the initial plans hadn't worked out. We were grappling with the problem when it was announced that the new cardinal of Chile, Monsignor Francisco Fresno, would be arriving in Santiago to replace Cardinal Silva Henríquez, who had retired at the age of seventy-five. Cardinal Silva had provided the Chilean people with a model of courage and struggle and he left a legacy of profound popular gratitude. The work he performed through the Vicariate of Solidarity had been a constant thorn in the side of the dictatorship.

And with good reason. His priests were working as carpenters, masons, and common laborers side by side with the inhabitants of the poorest *poblaciones*. Some of them had been killed by the police in street demonstrations. The government called for a suitably grand welcoming celebration for Cardinal Fresno. Even the state of siege was to be lifted for twenty-four hours. The new cardinal's political position was still uncertain, so most of us read the rousing welcome as Pinochet's celebration of Cardinal Silva Henríquez's retirement. The general himself left on a two-week trip to the north together with his family and a full complement of lesser ministers, probably so that neither he nor any of them would have to be present at a reception that could produce unpredictable reactions. Confused by the contradictory official actions, only a few thousand people showed up in the Plaza de Armas, while at least 6,000 had been expected.

It was not difficult to predict that a day of such official uncertainty would be propitious for taking the first batch of film out of the country. When Grazia arrived at the airport, it was more strictly patrolled than usual. But it was so crowded and chaotic that the police themselves helped her check her bags through on the same plane on which the cardinal had arrived so she would not miss her flight. Later that night we received the coded message from Valparaíso: *Grazia went to heaven.*

7

The Police on the Hunt:
The Circle Begins to Close

While I was filming in Concepción and Valparaíso without
having gotten in touch with her, Elena was getting more and
more worried. It was her duty to report my disappearance
but, knowing me for an incorrigible improviser, she allowed
more than the allotted time to pass. She waited all night
Saturday. When I hadn't appeared by Sunday, she contacted
whoever she thought might know where I had gone, but
nobody had any idea. Just when she had made up her mind
to make noon on Monday the deadline for sounding the
alarm, she saw me coming into the hotel, my face unshaven
and drawn with sleeplessness. She had been involved in many
important and dangerous missions but never before, she
swore to me, had she put up with so much from one of her
false, uncontrollable husbands. And this time she had good
reason to be angry with me. After countless efforts, unkept
appointments, and the most complex maneuvering, she had
finally arranged a meeting with the leaders of the underground Manuel Rodríguez Patriotic Front for that same
morning at eleven o'clock.

This was, without question, the riskiest of any of our undertakings, and the most important. The Front is made up almost exclusively of individuals who were just leaving elementary school when Pinochet seized power. It had unified the democratic opposition against the dictatorship, committing itself to the principle of inalienable human rights that informs all democracies. It took its name from a legendary figure of the Chilean independence movement of 1810 who possessed an uncanny ability to evade all surveillance, both inside the country and out. Rodríquez had managed to maintain constant communication between the liberation army operating in Mendoza on the Argentine side and the underground forces that continued resisting inside Chile after the patriots were defeated and power was retaken by the royalists. The situation at that time, in fact, bears a strong resemblance to current conditions in Chile.

The opportunity to interview leaders of the Patriotic Front would be a coup for any good journalist. How could I be an exception? After posting the members of the film crew at the various points agreed upon with the Front, I managed to get there myself at the last possible moment. I came along to a bus stop on Calle Providencia, carrying, as instructed, a copy of the day's *El Mercurio* and of the magazine *¿Que Pasa?* I was to do nothing until somebody approached and asked, "Are you going to the beach?" I was to answer, "No, to the zoo." This seemed like a ridiculous password. Nobody would think of going to the beach in the fall. But the two liaison officers of the Front told me later that, because it was absurd, nobody was likely to use it by chance. Ten minutes later, when I feared that I was already beginning to attract attention, I saw a very thin boy of medium height approach, limping on his left leg. He wore a beret which, as far as I was concerned, was a dead giveaway. He came over to me quite openly and I stepped forward to meet him before he could give the password.

"Is that the best disguise you could find?" I asked him, laughing. "Even I recognized you in that getup."

"Is it that easy to spot?"

"From a mile away."

He had a sense of humor and no conspiratorial airs, which eased tension from the start. As soon as he reached me, a bakery truck drew up to the curb beside me. I got into the seat next to the driver. We rode around the downtown area, picking up the members of the Italian crew at various prearranged spots. Later on, we were each dropped at one of five places, picked up again separately in other cars, and finally all brought together again in a pickup truck that was carrying cameras, lights, and sound equipment. I did not feel as though I were involved in a serious and important real-life adventure, but more as if I were playing at making a spy movie. The boy in the beret disappeared during one of the many maneuvers and I never saw him again. His place was taken by a driver who, although not opposed to kidding around, did his job with care. I sat beside him, and the rest of the crew climbed into the back of the truck.

"I'm going to take you boys for a little spin," he told us, "so you can get a whiff of the Chilean ocean."

He turned on the radio full blast and drove around, criss-crossing the city until I had no idea where we were. But that wasn't enough for him, and at one point he ordered us to close our eyes, using a Chilean expression I had forgotten. "Okay, kiddies," he said, "now you're going to make *tutito*."

When we didn't react immediately, he restated the order more forcefully. "All right, then, just shut your eyes and don't open them again until I tell you, because if you do, that'll be the end of the line."

He explained to us that whenever he drove people somewhere, they had to wear a special type of blind eyeglasses that look like sunglasses on the outside but are opaque, but he had forgotten the glasses. We would have to close our eyes. The Italians didn't understand his Chilean slang and I had to translate.

"Go to sleep," I told them.

They were even more confused. "Sleep?"

"Like you heard," I told them. "Lie down, close your eyes, and don't open them until I tell you to."

The Exact Distance: Ten Boleros

The film crew lay jammed together on the floor of the truck while I kept trying to identify whichever section of the city we were traveling through. The driver lost no time in pulling me up short. "What I said goes for you, too, *compañero*. So just make *tutito*."

I leaned back over the headrest of the seat, shut my eyes, and let myself be carried along on the flood of boleros that was pouring out of the radio. They were the most popular ones, sung by Raúl Chu Moreno, Lucho Gatica, Hugo Romani, and Leo Marini. Time passes and the generations succeed one another, but in Chilean hearts the bolero continues to reign supreme, more so than in any other country. Every once in a while, the truck stopped, indistinct mumbling could be heard, and then the driver's voice, "Okay, *ciao*, be seeing you." I imagined he must have been talking to other activists who were giving him instructions at key points along the route. At one point, thinking he wasn't watching me, I tried opening my eyes, only to discover that the rearview mirror was tilted in such a way that he could drive or talk to his contacts without taking his eyes off us.

"Naughty, naughty!" he scolded. "The next time anyone opens his eyes, the outing is over and everybody goes home."

I closed my eyes quickly and began to sing along with the radio: *Que te quiero, sabrás que te quiero*—"That I love you, you'll know that I love you." The Italians in the back joined in. The driver was pleased.

"That's it, kiddies, just sing. You sound real nice," he said. "And don't worry about a thing. You're in good hands."

Before I went into exile, there were certain places in Santiago I could identify with my eyes shut: the slaughterhouse, from the odor of the stale blood; the San Miguel section, from the smell of motor oils and railway materials. In Mexico, where I lived for many years, I could tell I was close to the Cuernavaca expressway from the unmistakable stench of the paper factory, or that I was nearing the Azcapotzalco barrio because of the smoke from its oil refinery. That afternoon in Santiago, I was unable to detect any familiar odor even though, just out of curiosity, I kept trying as we sang. After the tenth bolero, the truck stopped.

"No opening your eyes, yet," the driver warned us. "We're going to get out of the truck now, and then we're going to behave ourselves and walk, all holding hands, so you won't fall down and bust your asses."

We did as we were told and began climbing up and down a steep path of loose dirt that didn't seem to get much sunlight. At the end of it, we entered a place that was dark and less chilly, and smelled of fish. For a moment, I thought we might be in Valparaíso on the seacoast, though I didn't think the trip had taken that long. When the driver finally gave the order to open our eyes, we were in a narrow room with blank walls and cheap but well-cared-for furniture. A neatly dressed young man stood before me wearing a false mustache pasted on so carelessly that it made me laugh.

"You ought to fix yourself up," I told him. "Nobody's going to be taken in by that mustache."

He laughed too and pulled it off.

"I was in a big hurry," he explained.

The ice was broken and, bantering, we moved into the next room. A very young man, his head bandaged, lay on a bed, apparently drowsing. I then realized that we were in a

71

well-equipped clandestine hospital and that the patient was Fernando Larenas Seguel, the most wanted man in Chile.

He was a twenty-one-year-old activist in the Manuel Rodríguez Patriotic Front. Two weeks before, while driving home in his car in Santiago at one o'clock in the morning, alone and unarmed, he was suddenly surrounded by four men in civilian clothes carrying army rifles. Without giving an order or asking him a question, one of them fired at him through the windshield. Bullets penetrated his left arm and struck his skull. Forty-eight hours later, four officers of the Front rescued him at gunpoint from the Clínica de Nuestra Señora de las Nieves, where he lay in a coma under police guard, and brought him to one of the movement's four clandestine hospitals. On the day of our interview, he was recuperating, able to talk and answer our questions.

A few days later we were received by the high command of the Patriotic Front after following the same spy-movie precautions. Instead of an underground hospital, this time we were taken to a comfortable, pleasant middle-class home which had a large collection of classical records and an excellent library. Instead of filming these activists in hoods, which was our first idea, we decided to use different angles and lighting to protect their identity. The result, as may be seen in the finished documentary, was more convincing, more human, and much less intimidating than the usual interviews with underground leaders.

When the interviews with the various resistance leaders had been completed, Elena and I agreed that she should return to her regular activities in Europe, where she had been living for some time. Her political work was too important to permit her continued exposure to any more risks than were absolutely necessary. I had acquired enough experience up to that point to allow me to finish the remaining, and supposedly less dangerous, portions of the film without her help. I haven't seen her since, but as I watched her go off toward the subway station, once again in her plaid skirt and school-girl loafers, I realized that after so many hours of feigned love and real scares, I was going to miss her more than I had imagined.

In case the foreign film crews had to leave Chile for reasons beyond their control, or if they should be forbidden to work, a branch of the internal resistance was ready with a backup crew of young filmmakers from among their ranks. They turned out to be a huge success. This crew did the job as rapidly as the others and with equally good results; they were more enthusiastic, perhaps, because they were more politically involved in what they were doing. Their political organization assured us that they were not only completely trustworthy but thoroughly prepared to assume any risk. Toward the end, when we needed more people to film in the *poblaciones* and we no longer had enough foreigners, this crew took on the task of organizing more crews, and those, still others. In the end we had as many as six Chilean film crews working simultaneously in different places. To me these young people symbolized the determination of the new generation, which, acting slowly and without fanfare, has resolved to rescue Chile from the disaster of dictatorship. All of them, despite their youth, have more than just their vision of the future. They have a history of anonymous deeds and secret victories, which they guard with great modesty.

The Circle Begins to Close

The French crew returned to Santiago during the time we were interviewing the leadership of the Patriotic Front. They had successfully completed their schedule. This would be a vital part of the documentary since the north is a key area in the history of Chile's political development. From Luis Emilio Recabarren, founder of the first labor party at the beginning of the century, to Salvador Allende, ideological and political continuity can best be appreciated there. Commercial exploitation of the rich copper mines by the British in the last century gave birth to our own working class. The Chilean social movement that resulted was undoubtedly the most significant one of its kind in Latin America.

The report on its work by the director of the French crew, Jean Claude, was very extensive and detailed. I had to visualize everything as it would appear on screen in order to maintain the unity of the film, since there were no rushes. And there would be none until I was back in Madrid, too late to make adjustments. For security reasons we never had any set rendezvous places in Santiago, so Jean Claude and I were floating around the city that morning as we talked. We strolled through the downtown area, rode the less frequented bus routes, drank coffee in the busiest of the cafés, had shellfish and beer, and then, quite late in the evening, finding ourselves far from the hotel, we decided to take the subway back.

The construction of the subway was begun under President Frei, continued by Allende, and completed by the dictatorship, which also dedicated it, so it was a world I had not discovered until then. I was surprised at its cleanliness and efficiency and the readiness with which my countrymen had adapted to traveling underground. We had no cogent reason for requesting a permit to film in the subway, but the fact that the French had built it gave us the idea that Jean Claude and his crew might shoot there. We were discussing the plan as we came into Pedro Valdivia station. Going up the stairway on the way out, I sensed that we were being observed. In fact, a policeman in plain clothes was watching us so intently that when I turned my head our glances met.

It was easy for me to pick undercover police out of a crowd by then. Despite their dark blue overcoats and hair cropped short like army recruits, they still think they can pass as civilians. More than anything else, their way of staring at people gives them away. Chileans don't look at anybody in the street; they keep their eyes straight ahead when they walk or ride a bus. Consequently, when this heavyset man continued to look at me even though he realized he had been spotted, I knew he was a cop. Hands stuffed into the pockets of his heavy coat, cigarette dangling from his lips, he kept his left eye closed against the smoke in a pathetic imitation of a movie detective. He reminded me of "Fats" Romo, a government hit man who, posing as an ardent leftist, had turned in many underground activists who were later murdered.

I admit that my looking at him was a grave error but it was an unavoidable, unconscious impulse, not a voluntary act. The same instinctive reaction then made me look to my left and immediately to my right; I saw two more of them. "Talk to me about anything at all," I said to Jean Claude in a low voice. "Talk but don't gesticulate, don't look, don't do anything." He understood and we kept walking without hurrying until we reached the street. It was night, but the atmosphere had turned mild and clearer than on previous days, and there were many people on their way home along the Alameda. Separating from Jean Claude, I said to him, "Disappear. I'll get in touch with you later."

He took off to the right and I got lost among the people on the sidewalk. A taxi drove up alongside me at that very moment, as though sent by my mother, and I hopped into it. I could see the three men, who had just emerged from the subway, looking around in surprise, not knowing whether to go after Jean Claude or me, and I lost sight of them as the taxi pulled away. I got out four blocks ahead and took another taxi in the opposite direction and then another and another until it seemed impossible that I was being trailed. The only thing I didn't understand, and still don't, is why they should have wanted to follow us. Finally I stopped at the first movie theater I saw and went in without even looking to see what it was showing, convinced, as usual, out of pure professional prejudice, that there could be no safer or more suitable place in which to think.

"How Do You Like My Fanny, Sir?"

It turned out that the program consisted of a movie and a live show. I had hardly settled back in my seat when the picture ended, the houselights came up to half intensity, and the master of ceremonies went into a long pitch about the show. I was still so upset that I kept glancing back at the door to see if I had been followed. My neighbors also began turning around with the curiosity that is almost a law of human behavior. In a place like that, though, each of them might well have had his own reason to worry about being discovered. Everything about it was garish: the decor, the lights, the movie, the striptease, and particularly the audience, everyone with the look of a fugitive from God knows where. Any policeman would have taken that audience for a roundup of suspicious characters.

The management encouraged the impression of a forbidden spectacle. The master of ceremonies introduced the strippers from the stage with descriptions that would have been more appropriate for the special dishes on a menu. Each girl made her entrance more naked than when she came into the world, her body doctored to lend charms it did not naturally possess. After the opening parade, a dark girl with enormous curves and bulges remained alone on the stage, wriggling her body and lip-synching to the voice of Rocío Durcal on a recording played at ear-splitting volume. I had just decided that I could risk leaving, when she came down from the stage with a microphone trailing a long cord and began asking the audience smutty questions meant to be amusing. I was waiting for the right moment to get out when I was suddenly dazzled by the spotlight.

"You, sir, with the cute bald spot . . ."

She wasn't referring to me, of course, but to my other self. Unfortunately, I had to answer for him. She came so close to me with the microphone that I could smell the onions on her breath.

"How do you like my hips?"

"Very nice," I answered into the microphone. "What do you want me to say?"

She then turned her back to me and waved her rear practically in my face.

"And my fanny, sir, what do you think of it?"

"Terrific," I said. "Really something."

After each answer canned guffaws came over the loud-speakers as in U.S. television programs. All the people in the theater looked as though they wished they could make themselves invisible. The stripper came even closer to me, writhed a bit in my face and displayed a real mole, black and hairy as a spider, on one of her buttocks.

"Naturally," I said, "you're very pretty all over."

"And what would you do with me if I offered to spend the night in bed with you? Come on, now, tell me all."

"Well, I don't know what to tell you. But I'd really enjoy that."

The torture was relentless. To make matters worse, I had forgotten to talk like an Uruguayan and then tried to make a last-minute adjustment. Imitating my indeterminate accent, she then asked me where I was from. When I told her, she exclaimed, "The Uruguayans are very good in bed. What about you?"

I had no alternative but to get stuffy.

"Please, don't ask me any more questions," I said.

Realizing that I was a lost cause, she looked around for another victim. As soon as I felt that I could make my escape unnoticed, I left as rapidly as I could and returned to my hotel, convinced that there had been nothing accidental about what happened that evening.

8

Get Ready.
There's a General Willing
to Spill Everything

Apart from Elena's contacts, I had begun working with sympathetic friends of my own from the old days who helped me set up the Chilean crews and made it possible for us to move about freely in the *poblaciones*. The first person I looked up when I returned from Concepción was Eloisa, a beautiful and elegant woman married to a well-known businessman.

Eloisa and I originally met through political activity at the university and we became close friends during Salvador Allende's last presidential campaign, for which we did propaganda work together. A few days after my arrival, I happened to hear that she was the star of a leading public relations firm. Before approaching her, I made an anonymous telephone call to her to make sure she was the same person. The soft, self-assured voice that answered seemed like hers but something about her diction threw me off. To make sure, I took a seat in a coffee shop on Calle Huérfanos from which I could observe the entrance to her building. It was she, even more beautiful and elegant than before. I also noted that she had no chauffeur driving her flashy silver BMW 635, as might be expected of the wife of an influential bourgeois. I dropped her a one-line note: "Antonio is here and would like to see you." That was the alias I used in the days of the university political struggles and I was sure she would not have forgotten.

She had not forgotten. At one o'clock sharp the silver shark glided slowly down Calle Apoquindo and stopped in front of the Renault agency. I jumped in and closed the door. She looked at me in consternation until she heard my laugh, which she hadn't forgotten either.

"You're out of your mind!" she said.

"Did you ever have reason to doubt it?" I answered.

We went to the restaurant where I had gone alone on my first day in Santiago, but the entrance was boarded up and bore a sign that read like an epitaph: CLOSED FOREVER. We ended up at a French restaurant in the same area. It was a pleasant place across the street from the city's best-known motel. Eloisa amused herself by identifying the cars of her customers who were making use of its facilities as we lunched and I couldn't get over her uninhibited sense of fun.

I had no hesitation about telling her the reason for my clandestine visit and asked for her help in making certain contacts that would probably be less dangerous for a woman protected as she was by her class status. This was at a time when we were having trouble filming in the *poblaciones* because we lacked the proper political sponsorship. I figured she could help locate some mutual friends from the Popular Unity days whom I had lost track of in the twilight of exile.

Not only did she accept the task with enthusiasm, but she accompanied me herself to secret meetings for three nights in sections of the city where it would be less dangerous to appear in a car like hers. "Impossible to imagine that a BMW 635 could be an enemy of the dictatorship," she commented with satisfaction.

In fact, the BMW saved me from being arrested one night when a blackout caught Eloisa and me at a secret meeting. The resistance had warned us that they were going to interrupt power lines several times that day. First they would create a forty-minute blackout. Later there would be another of one hour, and finally one that would leave Santiago without electricity for two to three days. This meeting was scheduled early because the armed forces get into a state bordering on hysteria during blackouts and the dragnet on the streets becomes indiscriminate and brutal. But something went wrong and the first blackout hit while we were still talking.

The political people in charge of the meeting decided that Eloisa and I should leave the moment the blackout was over. As soon as the lights came back on we drove off on an unpaved road that ran along the edge of a mountain. As we rounded a curve, we suddenly found ourselves in the midst of a blockage of security vehicles lined up on both sides of the road, forming a kind of tunnel. Men in civilian clothes were carrying submachine guns. Eloisa was going to stop but I told her not to.

"But we're supposed to stop," she said.

"Keep going," I told her. "Don't get nervous, keep on talking, keep laughing, and don't come to a stop until you are ordered to. And don't worry, my papers are in order."

As I said it, I touched my pocket and my insides turned to ice. I had not brought the envelope with my identification. One of the men crossed the road in front of us with his hand raised. Eloisa stopped the car. He turned a flashlight on our faces, ran the beam over the inside of the car, and waved us on without a word. Eloisa was right. It was impossible to be suspicious of an automobile like hers.

A Grandmother with a Parachute

It was around then that Eloisa introduced me to her mother-in-law, whom we both decided to call Clemencia Isaura for reasons neither of us can remember. We arrived unannounced at her sumptuous residence, No. 727, in the exclusive heights section of Santiago at five o'clock in the afternoon. Clemencia was a seventy-year-old widow who fought loneliness by watching television sitcoms and dreamt of being the heroine of a real-life adventure someday. We found her in her customary placid mood, having a cup of tea and English biscuits as she watched television, the room reverberating with the roar of gunfire. She was wearing a beautifully tailored gray suit, hat, and gloves. It was her habit to have tea at five o'clock sharp, dressed for a party even though she was alone. However, those customs out of an English novel did not really suit her personality. When she was already married and the mother of several children, she became a glider pilot in Canada and later racked up an impressive record as a parachutist.

When she heard that we had come to her about an important and dangerous clandestine mission, she said, "That's splendid! Life is so dull here that one does little more than worry about makeup and clothes, and for no good reason." When I asked that she help me find five old friends and comrades, the request came as somewhat of a disappointment.

"Too bad," she said, "I was hoping you were at least going to ask me to plant bombs."

I preferred not to use the usual resistance channels to search for these five men. None of them was exiled. One was the man who on the day of the military coup notified Ely that they were going to execute me in front of the Chile Films building. The second had been in a concentration camp during the first year of the dictatorship. When he came out, he returned to what was apparently an ordinary way of life, but he was actually a dedicated political worker. The third had spent some time in Mexico, where he contacted Chilean exiles, returned with his papers in order, and joined the resistance. The fourth, with whom I had been at the theater school and later in films and television, is currently an active labor leader. The fifth was a truck driver; he had been in Italy for two years and was, therefore, perfectly qualified to help us with the film. All five had changed addresses, jobs, and identities, and I had no clue as to their whereabouts. More than a thousand Chileans live like that and are active in the resistance under a different identity from the one they had in 1973. The challenge for Clemencia Isaura was to locate the end of the thread and find her way to the spool.

The initial contacts she developed would be vital for gauging the attitudes of my old friends before I revealed to them that I was in Chile and needed their help. I never found out exactly how Clemencia accomplished what she did. We had barely any time together to talk before I had to leave Chile, though the one thing she did say was that nothing she had ever seen on television was as exciting as the experiences she had finding my five lost friends.

I know that she walked those slum barrios for days on end asking here, checking there, on the basis of the sketchy information I was able to provide. I had warned her to dress so that she would blend in with the people there, but she paid no attention and strolled the rugged paths of the Santiago slaughterhouse district as though she were on her way to have tea and English biscuits. Those who were approached by that elegant old lady inquiring about vague addresses with suspicious curiosity must have wondered at the incongruity of her mission. But her irresistible charm and genuine warmth won immediate confidence. At the end of one week she had not only located three of the missing persons but had invited them all to dinner at No. 727, where she entertained them as elegantly as if it had been a high-society party.

The Long Pursuit of General Electric

At the same time that Clemencia Isaura was working, I spent my time when I wasn't filming taking advantage of Eloisa's help in making contacts at the upper echelons of power. One night while she and I were having supper in a posh restaurant and waiting for an emissary (who never showed up), two generals draped in medals entered. Eloisa waved to them with such an air of familiarity that I had sudden, serious suspicions about her. One of the generals came over to our table and stood chatting with Eloisa for a few minutes, paying absolutely no attention to me. I had no idea what his rank was because I have never learned to distinguish between the stars of generals and those of hotels. As he walked to his table she lowered her voice and mentioned that her work had made it possible for her to make some very interesting contacts with various high-ranking army officers.

In Eloisa's opinion, one of the factors that kept Pinochet in power was that he had retired the officers of his own generation and retained a high command of younger officers who had always been far below him in rank, who were not his friends, who barely knew him, and who for the most part obeyed him slavishly. At the same time this made him vulnerable. Many of these new officers felt that they should not be held responsible for Allende's assassination, the usurpation of power, and the bloody years that followed. They felt that their hands were clean and hoped to reach an agreement one day with the civilians for a return to democracy. After my astonished reaction, she went even further: there was at least one general ready to make public revelations regarding the deep divisions in the structure of the armed forces!

"He is bursting to talk," she told me.

This piece of news shook me up. The prospect of introducing spectacular testimony like that into my documentary completely changed the outlook for the next few days. The unfortunate part was that Eloisa could not run the risk of making the initial contact, nor would she have time to attempt it, because she was leaving in a few days on a three-month trip to Europe with her husband.

A few days later, however, Clemencia Isaura summoned me to her house and handed me a password that Eloisa had sent; it would enable me to meet General Electric, as we had named the dissident officer. She also gave me a small electronic chess game that I was to take with me the following day to San Francisco Church at five o'clock in the afternoon.

I couldn't remember the last time I had been inside a church. Men and women were sitting around reading newspapers and books, knitting, playing solitaire, doing crossword puzzles. Not until then did I understand why Eloisa had supplied me with a chess board, which had hardly seemed appropriate. People were also standing in the afternoon shadows, silent and brooding, like those I had observed on the night of my arrival. Actually the Chileans had been like that before Popular Unity, too. The big change came when Allende's campaign got under way and it appeared that he might win. His victory transformed the country overnight. We sang in the streets, painted on the walls, held theater performances, and projected movies outdoors, everybody milling around in huge throngs, letting go of our joy.

After two days of playing chess with my Uruguayan self in the church, I heard a woman's voice close to me, whispering. I was seated and she had knelt at the bench behind me, so she spoke practically into my ear.

"Don't look at me or say anything," she told me in a voice suitable for a confessional. Memorize the telephone number and password I am going to give you, then wait for at least fifteen minutes after I have left before you leave."

Not until she had risen and walked toward the main altar did I realize that she was a young and very beautiful nun. I needed to remember only the password because I had marked out the telephone number on the chessboard with the pawns. I assumed that this would give me access to General Electric, but the cards were stacked differently. On the days that followed, my anxiety mounted. Each time I called the number I was given the same answer: "Tomorrow."

Who Can Figure Out the Police?

When least expected, Jean Claude brought bad news. He had read a *France Presse* release datelined a week earlier in Santiago and published in Paris that reported that three members of an Italian film crew working in Chile under suspicious circumstances had been arrested while photographing in the *población* of La Legua without a permit.

Frankie thought we had hit bottom. I tried to take the news calmly. Like the Italians, Jean Claude was unaware that other crews were working with me. His alarm was purely inferential: if somebody in a situation similar to his had been arrested, then the same could happen to him. I tried to reassure him that we would not be affected.

As soon as he left, I went to check up on the Italians and found Grazia back from Europe and all of them safe and sound where they were supposed to be. However, Ugo confirmed that the wire story had also appeared in Italy, although the Italian news agency retracted it later. The worst part was that the false story carried their real names and had spread rapidly. Santiago under the dictatorship was a beehive of rumors. Stories would come to life, be propagated in astonishing profusion several times a day, and always with a basis in truth, and then fade away. The story about the Italians was no exception. There had been so much talk that when the crew arrived at a reception in the Italian embassy the night before, they were greeted by no less a personage than the head of the General Office of Communications, who said in a voice loud enough for all the guests to hear: "Look, here are our three prisoners for you."

Grazia had had the impression that they were being followed even before she heard about the wire story. When the group returned to the hotel after the embassy party, it appeared that their suitcases and papers had been searched. It might have been an illusion prompted by their uneasiness, but it could also have been a warning. In any case, there was reason to believe something was up.

In case I were arrested I stayed up all that night writing a letter to the president of the Supreme Court, who still retained some independence under the military dictatorship. In it, I acknowledged my clandestine return to my country. Writing the letter was not a sudden impulse but something I had considered for some time, which had become more urgent now that the circle had begun to close around us. At first I conceived of the letter as a single dramatic sentence, like a castaway's message in a bottle thrown into the sea, but as I set about writing it, I realized that it was necessary to give my action political and human significance so that it would also express the feelings of the thousands of Chileans trying to survive the plague of exile. I made many false starts and tore up many sheets of paper there in the gloomy hotel room which was itself a place of private exile in my own land. By the time I finished, the church bells ringing the Mass had already shattered the silence of curfew and the first light of morning was making its way through the shadows of a new day in that unforgettable autumn.

9

Not Even My Own Mother Recognizes Me

There was good reason to fear that the police were aware of my presence in Chile and knew what we were doing there. After nearly a month in Santiago, the film crews had been seen in public more times than was advisable, we had been in contact with all sorts of people, and many now knew that it was I who was directing the film. I had become so forgetful of my new identity that I was neglecting to speak with a Uruguayan accent and, as myself, I had grown sloppy about passwords and contacts and I took risks with my own safety.

In the beginning, meetings were held in cars cruising the city without fixed destinations. Every four or five blocks the car was changed. This procedure became so complicated that we sometimes incurred risks worse than those we were trying to avoid. One night, for example, I got out of a car on the corner of Providencia and Los Leones, where I was to be picked up five minutes later by a blue Renault 12 with a sticker of the Society for the Protection of Animals on the windshield. It arrived so punctually, so Renault 12, and so blue that I didn't bother to look for the sticker and just climbed right into the backseat. A woman was sitting there, no longer young but still very beautiful, dripping with jewels, provocatively perfumed, wearing a pink mink coat that must have cost two or three times as much as the car itself. She was an unmistakable but rarely encountered example of the Santiago upper crust. Her jaw dropped in astonishment as she watched me clamber in, so I hastened to reassure her by giving the password: "Where can I buy an umbrella at this hour?"

The uniformed chauffeur turned around and barked, "Get out of this car or I'll call the police!"

A quick glance at the windshield was enough to verify that there was no sticker there, and I was suddenly sickened by the absurdity of the situation. "Excuse me," I mumbled, "I seem to have gotten into the wrong car." But by now the woman had recovered her composure. She took hold of my arm, reassured the chauffeur in a clear voice, and then asked him, "Would the Paris department store still be open?"

The chauffeur replied that he thought it would be and she insisted on driving me there for the umbrella. She was as charming and warm as she was beautiful and one would have wished to linger in the pleasure of her company, forgetting, for just one night, repression, politics, even art. She dropped me at the entrance to the Paris department store with an apology for not going with me to buy the umbrella because she was already late in picking up her husband, with whom she was going to attend a concert.

Such were the dangers of routine. We were using fewer and fewer cryptic passwords for identification in clandestine meetings. We would make friends with emissaries the moment they arrived and, instead of getting down to business at once, took time to comment on the political situation, the film and literary scene, and mutual friends I wanted to see despite warnings to resist such temptations. One emissary, perhaps to reinforce the appearance of innocence, arrived at our appointment with his child who, wide-eyed with excitement, asked me, "Are you the one who's making a picture about Superman?" And so I began to realize that it was quite possible to live secretly in Chile, as many hundreds of returned exiles do, carrying on their daily life without the degree of anxiety I experienced on arrival. In fact, I felt this so strongly that had it not been for the responsibility of the film, an obligation to my country, my friends, and myself, I would have changed profession and milieu and remained in Santiago wearing my own face.

But in view of the suspicion that the police were watching us, a modicum of prudence forced me to maintain my disguise. Authorization to film inside the Moneda Palace had been inexplicably postponed several times and was still pending. Also, Puerto Montt and the Central Valley still remained to be done, to say nothing of the tantalizing possibility of the interview with General Electric. Furthermore, I wanted to shoot the Central Valley myself since it was the region where I was born and lived until adolescence. My mother was still there in the poor village of Palmilla, but I had been strictly warned to stay away from her on this trip for the obvious reasons of security.

The first thing I did was to reorganize the work of the foreign crews so that they could finish up as rapidly as possible with a minimum of risk and return to their respective countries. Only the Italians would remain for the filming of the Moneda Palace. The French crew was scheduled to leave right after shooting the hunger march, which would take place in the next few days.

The Dutch crew was waiting for me in Puerto Montt to film nearly as far as the Antarctic Circle. When that was over, they would leave Chile for Argentina at the border town of Bariloche. When the three crews had left Chile, eighty percent of the film would have been shot and would have arrived safely in Madrid for developing. I was to find that Ely had been so efficient that the picture was ready for cutting by the time I reached Spain.

Littín Came, Filmed, and Went Away

Considering how uncertain things were in those days, it seemed advisable for Frankie and me to get out of the country and reenter immediately with extreme caution. The trip to Puerto Montt provided the ideal opportunity to do this because I could get there as easily from Chile as from Argentina. So I asked the Dutch crew to wait for me in Puerto Montt and notified one of the Chilean crews to be in the Colchagua Valley, in the center of the country, and Frankie and I left by plane for Buenos Aires. I had called the magazine *Análisis* a few hours before and gave a reporter, Patricia Collier, a long interview on my clandestine visit to Santiago. It appeared two days after my staged departure from Chile with my photo on the cover and a title that had a touch of Roman mockery: "Littín Came, Filmed, and Went Away."

To make everything appear even more authentic, Clemencia Isaura drove Frankie and me to the Pudahuel airport in her car and said good-bye to us with overacted tears and embraces. So we left as ostentatiously as possible but within sight of our friends in the resistance who could have sounded the alarm if we had been arrested. The departure proved to us that we were not under surveillance at the airport. Also, our exit would be on record in case of subsequent investigation so that the police would believe we were no longer in the country.

I used my legitimate passport for identification in Buenos Aires to avoid committing an illegal act in a friendly country. As I was about to present it at the Argentine immigration window, an unforeseen problem occurred to me: the real passport photograph, taken before my transformation, didn't look anything like the new me. With my plucked eyebrows, large bald spot, and thick glasses, I was almost unrecognizable. I had been warned at the outset that it would be just as difficult to regain my own personality as it had been to assume the new one, but when I most needed to keep this in mind I had forgotten it. Fortunately, the officials in Buenos Aires did not look at my face, and so I lived through yet another drama of not being able to be myself, even though this time I could have been.

In Buenos Aires, Frankie had to coordinate on the phone with Ely in Madrid the many details of the work that remained, so we separated there, having arranged to meet again in Santiago. I flew to Mendoza, still in Argentine territory, to take some of the shots we had planned of the Chilean cordillera. It was easy enough because one enters Chile from Mendoza through a tunnel where controls are relatively lax. I went across alone on foot with a light sixteen-millimeter camera, did what was necessary on the other side, and was driven back by a kind Chilean policeman who took pity on a poor Uruguayan newspaperman who had no way to get back to Argentina.

From Mendoza, I went on to Bariloche, the other border point farther south. A decrepit old ship crammed with Argentine, Uruguayan, Brazilian, and Chilean tourists took me from there to the Chilean border through a polar landscape of ice cliffs and stormy seas. For the last leg of the trip to Puerto Montt, I took a ferry with broken windows through which the freezing wind entered, howling like a pack of wolves. There was nowhere to protect oneself from the frightful cold and nothing to drink, not a cup of coffee, not a glass of wine, nothing. However, I had calculated correctly. If my departure had been noted by the police in the airport, they would hardly have expected me to reenter Chile the next day from a point more than 600 miles from Santiago.

Shortly after we reached the border checkpoint, some 300 passports were collected from the passengers, given scarcely a cursory glance, stamped, and returned. The Chileans, however, were checked against a long list of names of exiles forbidden to enter that was posted on the wall next to the immigration inspectors. For the foreigners, me among them, the border crossing was uneventful until two *carabineros*, whom I did not recognize as such because of their arctic clothing, ordered us to open our luggage. It was clearly a thorough inspection but I was unconcerned since I thought I was carrying nothing out of keeping with my false identity. When I opened my bag, however, the empty Gitanes packages, many with shooting notes written all over them, spilled out and scattered all over the floor.

I had arrived with a stock of Gitanes sufficient for two months and didn't dare throw away the large, empty packages made of hard cardboard that might have been conspicuous in Chile and could have provided a trail for the police. I kept them in my pockets after smoking the cigarettes as I worked and then put them away in different places, saving the packages for the notes scribbled on them. Finally, there came a time when it must have looked as if I had a magic act, with so many empty cigarette packages stashed in the pockets of all the clothes in the closet, under the mattress, in my luggage, waiting for the time when I could think of a safe way to get rid of them. So I fell victim to the same kind of absurd predicament as prisoners who dig an escape tunnel and then can't figure out how to dispose of the dirt.

Every time I packed to change hotels, I would ponder the problem. And each time I could come up with no better solution than to take the packages along in my suitcase because, if I were surprised while trying to destroy them, it might seem more suspicious than it actually was. I thought of getting rid of them in Argentina but things happened too quickly there. I hadn't needed to open my bags until I was obliged to at the southern border and noted with horror the *carabineros'* expressions of surprise and suspicion as they watched me scrambling to pick up the tumbling, scattering packages.

"They're empty," I said.

They didn't believe me, of course. While the younger of the two men occupied himself with the other passengers, the older one opened each package and examined it inside and out, trying to make some sense of my notes. I had a moment of inspiration.

"Those are just little poems I make up every once in a while," I said.

He continued his examination in silence, finally looking me squarely in the face as if hoping to gather some clue to the mystery of the empty cigarette packages from my expression.

"You can keep them if you'd like," I offered.

"What would I do with them?" he replied.

Then he helped me put them all neatly back into the suitcase and proceeded to the next passenger. I was so confused that it didn't occur to me to dump them in the trash right then and there before the *carabineros'* eyes, instead of continuing to drag them around with me for the rest of the trip. Back in Madrid, I wouldn't let Ely destroy them, so closely did I identify them with all my trying experiences in Chile.

"Take a Picture of the Country's Future"

The Dutch crew was waiting in Puerto Montt as planned. We were to film there not only for the indescribable beauty of the landscape, but because of the region's importance in Chile's recent history. It had been an arena of constant struggle. During Eduardo Frei's administration, the repression there was so brutal that the last remaining progressive sectors of the government withdrew from it. After that, it became clear to the democratic left that the future of the region, and of the entire country, lay in unity. This triggered the rapid and inexorable process that culminated in the election of Salvador Allende as president.

When filming was finished in Puerto Montt, and with it the entire schedule for the south, the Dutch crew left for Buenos Aires via Bariloche, with a considerable amount of film for Ely in Madrid. I went on alone to Talca by a comfortable night train on which nothing of moment took place except for an encounter with a roast chicken that returned unscathed to the kitchen. It had been impossible to make so much as a dent in its armored carcass. In Talca, I rented a car and went to San Fernando in the heart of the Colchagua Valley.

The town square was exactly as I remembered it. There wasn't a tree or a stone in a wall that didn't take me back to my childhood. Most of all, the old schoolhouse where I learned to read and write. I sat on a bench to take photos that I could use in my film. The square gradually filled with boisterous children on their way to school. Some stopped and posed in front of the camera, others tried to put their hands over the lens. One little girl did some dance steps so expertly that I asked her to repeat them against a better background. Just then, several boys came over, sat down next to me, and said, "How about taking a picture of the country's future?"

The remark was surprising because it echoed something I had written down on one of my Gitanes packages: *I think it would be impossible to find anyone in Chile who doesn't have his own idea of the future.* This is particularly true of the children who, although they belong to a generation that never knew a different country, have firm convictions concerning their destiny.

I had arranged to meet the Chilean crew at eleven o'clock

in the morning at the Maquis bridge. I arrived punctually at the right bank and saw the cameras set up along the opposite side. It was a clear morning, perfumed with the scent of thyme, and I was feeling secure and less of an exile in my own land now that I had taken off my other self's necktie and English suit and was back to my sheepskin jacket and jeans. The pleasure of two days' growth of beard, acquired while traveling from Buenos Aires, added to my recovered sense of self.

When I was certain that the cameraman had spotted me in his viewfinder, I got out of the car and crossed the bridge slowly to give him time to film me. Then I greeted the members of the crew one by one, buoyed by the enthusiasm and precocious maturity of those boys. Amazingly, they were fifteen, sixteen, and nineteen years old. Ricardo, the director, was twenty-one. The others called him "the old man." Nothing encouraged me as much during that time as having gained the confidence of that crew.

Leaning on the railing of the bridge, we planned the shooting right there and immediately went to work. I must confess that my thoughts that day strayed a bit from our main purpose and went trailing after my childhood memories. So I began with shots of that same bridge where, when I was about twelve, a group of rowdy girl cousins pushed me into the water to teach me to swim, or sink.

In the course of the day's work, though, the basic intent of the trip reasserted itself. The San Fernando Valley is a vast agricultural expanse where the peasants who had been serfs since time immemorial became, under Allende's Popular Unity government, citizens whose rights were respected for the first time. The region used to be a stronghold of the feudal oligarchy which was able to decide elections with the captive votes of its vassals. The first large-scale peasant strike was organized there during the Christian Democratic administration of Eduardo Frei, with the personal participation of

Salvador Allende. When Allende later came to power, he stripped the landlords of their excessive privileges and organized the peasants into active, interdependent communities. Now, as a symbol of Chile's historical step backward, Pinochet's summer home stands in this same valley.

I couldn't leave without getting some footage of the statue of Don Nicolás Palacios, author of *The Chilean Race*. In that outlandish book, Palacios argues that the true Chileans—those antedating the great Basque, Italian, Arab, French, and German immigrations—were direct descendants of the Hellenes of ancient Greece and were, therefore, preordained to be the guiding force in Latin America and to lead the world to truth and salvation. I was born nearby and saw that statue several times a day, but nobody could ever tell me who he was. Palacios's most ardent admirer, Augusto Pinochet, rescued him from historical limbo by erecting another statue of him in the heart of Santiago.

We finished shooting toward evening, with barely enough time to cover the ninety miles back to Santiago before curfew. All the members of the crew made their way straight home except Ricardo, who stayed with me in my car. We took a long detour along the coast to select locations for the next day's filming and were so engrossed in our work that we passed through four police checkpoints without even getting nervous. However, after the first one, I did take the precaution of changing from the informal garb of Miguel Littín, film director, to that of his stuffy Uruguayan counterpart. We completely lost track of time and then felt a wave of panic when we realized that it was already midnight, half an hour past the beginning of curfew. I told Ricardo to get off the main highway immediately and onto a dirt road that I remembered as if I had been on it only the day before. I directed him to turn left, go over the bridge, drive to the right into a scarcely distinguishable alley, then to switch off the headlights and continue along another unpaved road with sharp curves and sudden drops. After that maze, we drove into a sleeping village, rousing all the dogs as we approached and came to a stop in front of my mother's house.

Ricardo refused to believe, and still won't, that this was not premeditated. I swear it wasn't. The truth is that the moment I realized we were violating curfew, the only solution that occurred to me was to hide on a back road until dawn. It wasn't until we had left the highway that I recognized the dirt road of my childhood, the barking dogs on the other side of the bridge, the smell of the ashes of smothered kitchen fires, and was unable to resist the rash impulse to surprise my mother.

"You Must Be a Friend of My Children's"

Palmilla, a village of 400 inhabitants, hasn't changed since I was a boy. My paternal grandfather—a Palestinian born in Beith Sagur—and my maternal grandfather—the Greek, Cristos Cucumides—were among the first immigrants who settled around the railroad station at the turn of the century. Palmilla's only importance was its location at the terminus of the train that now links Santiago and the coast. It was the place where passengers changed and merchandise was loaded or unloaded. The village enjoyed a temporary prosperity from the constant coming and going. Later on, when the railroad was extended to the sea, the station was maintained as an obligatory ten-minute stop for the locomotives to take on water; this frequently stretched into a day-long enterprise, the trains whistling to announce their arrival as they passed by the house of my Arab grandmother, Matilde. The village never amounted to more than it is now, one long street with some scattered houses and a side road with even fewer buildings. Farther below the village is a place called La Calera, famous because every family there makes its own excellent wine and all travelers are invited to sample the wines and judge which is best. At one time, La Calera became a paradise for drunkards from all over Chile.

Matilde brought the first picture magazines to Palmilla and I have had an insatiable appetite for them ever since. She would also let circuses, traveling theaters, and puppeteers use the orchard across from her house. It was there that I saw the rare movies that would make it to such out-of-the-way villages as ours, and where I discovered my vocation after seeing my first picture, at five years of age, seated in my grandmother's lap. It was *Genoveva of Bravante* and I can still remember my reaction. I was terrified and it took years before I understood how it was possible for horses to gallop and giant heads to appear on a sheet that hung from the trees.

The house Ricardo and I came to that night, originally my Greek grandmother's, is where my mother, Cristina Cucumides, now lives and where I spent my childhood until adolescence. It was built long ago in the traditional style of rural Chile: long corridors, dark halls with a labyrinth of rooms off them, and a huge kitchen, with the stables and pasture close by. The house is in an area called Los Naranjos, where bougainvillea grows profusely and the heavy fragrance of bitter oranges hangs in the air.

I was so overwhelmed at being home that I was on my way out of the car door before we had stopped. I walked through the empty passageways and crossed the dark yard, greeted only by a foolish dog that tangled itself up in my legs, and I kept on without seeing any sign of human presence. Each step brought back a memory, a particular hour of the day, a forgotten odor. At the end of the long hall, I poked my head in the doorway of the living room, dimly lighted by a single bulb, and there was my mother.

It was a strange sight. The living room was large, the ceilings high, the walls bare, and there was no furniture but the armchair in which my mother was sitting, her back to the door, a brazier beside her, and another identical chair occupied by her brother, my Uncle Pablo. They sat in silence, an expression of trusting contentment on their faces, as though they were watching television. But they weren't looking at anything. I walked toward them not trying to be quiet, but seeing that they didn't move, I said, "Doesn't anybody say hello in this house?"

My mother then stood up.

"You must be a friend of my children's," she said. "Let me give you a hug."

Uncle Pablo hadn't seen me since I left Chile twelve years before and didn't even move in his chair. My mother and I had been together in Madrid the September before, but even after rising to embrace me she still did not recognize me. I then took her by both arms and tried to shake her gently out of her bewilderment.

Fixing my eyes on hers, I said, "Take a good look at me now, Cristina. It's me."

She peered at me again more intently but still couldn't place me.

"No," she said, "I don't know who you are."

"How can you not know me?" I said, bursting into laughter. "I'm your son, Miguel."

She looked at me again and the color drained from her face.

"Ay!" she said. "I'm going to faint."

As I moved to keep her from falling, my Uncle Pablo stood up in the same state of consternation.

"This is the last thing I expected to see," he said. "I can die in peace, now, right this minute."

I rushed over to embrace him. He was like a little bird, his hair all white, wrapped in an old man's blanket, even though he was only five years older than I. He married once, separated, and then came to live at my mother's house, where he has stayed. He was always a solitary person who seemed like an old man even when he was a boy.

"Don't give me that, Uncle," I said. "You wouldn't pull such a stunt on me. Better bring out a bottle of wine and let's celebrate my return."

My mother interrupted us with one of her supernatural revelations.

"I have the *mastul* ready," she said.

I couldn't believe it until I actually saw it in the kitchen. *Mastul* is a dish reserved in Greek homes exclusively for the most festive occasions because its preparation is extremely laborious. Made of lamb, chickpeas, and semolina balls, it is similar to Arab couscous. This was the first time my mother had prepared it that year—and for no special reason. It was pure inspiration.

Ricardo ate with us and then went off to bed so that we could be alone. My uncle retired soon after, and my mother and I stayed up talking until dawn. She and I had always talked a great deal, more like friends, because our age difference was not so great. At sixteen she married my father and I was born a year later, so I can remember very well what she was like at twenty. Very pretty and gentle, she would play with me as though I were one of her dolls and not her child.

She was radiant at my return but a bit disheartened by my clothing. "You look like a priest," she said to me. I did not tell her the reason, or why and how I had entered Chile, so that she would believe I was there legally. I preferred to keep her in the dark about my adventure so as not to upset her, of course, but particularly not to endanger her.

Just before dawn she took me by the hand and led me across the yard without explaining, carrying a lighted candle in a candlestick, as in a Dickens novel. It was the greatest, the best surprise of my trip. At the rear of the yard was the study of my house in Santiago, just as I had left it when I went into exile, with its entire contents.

After the soldiers had searched my house for the last time, and I was in Mexico with Ely and the children, my mother hired an architect friend who took my study apart board by board and built an exact replica of it at the family house in Palmilla. It was as if I had never gone away. All my life's papers, boyhood plays, outlines of film scripts, scenic designs, were there just as I had left them, even in the same disorder. So familiar was the atmosphere of that room, the smell in the air, that I even had the feeling it was the same day and the same hour as when I stood looking at my study, saying good-bye to it for good. Twelve years later, as I looked at it again in the garden, I couldn't be sure whether my mother had created that painstaking reconstruction so that I would not miss my former home if I were to return one day, or whether it was left as is to remember me by, should I die in exile.

10

Happy Ending Courtesy
of the Police

Coming back to Santiago this time was a return to the whirl-
wind. The feeling that the circle was tightening had become
almost palpable. The police had savagely beaten the partic-
ipants in the hunger march, including several members of
our crew. The people we were working with had the impression that nobody had believed our departure ploy. Even Clemencia Isaura was convinced that we were innocents walking
into the lion's den. Efforts to make contact with the dissident
General Electric were frustrated by the constantly repeated
"Call tomorrow." Then suddenly the Italian crew was notified that a permit had been issued to film in the Moneda
Palace at 11:00 A.M. the next day.

It was impossible not to believe it was a trap. I was willing
to take the risk but I couldn't assume the responsibility of
ordering the Italians to go into the presidential offices without knowing whether we were heading into an ambush. On
their own the crew decided to go ahead, with full knowledge
of the dangers involved. The French crew had no reason to
remain in Santiago. We held an emergency meeting and I

told them to get on the first available flight, taking all their exposed film along to be sent to Madrid. They left the same afternoon that the Italians were filming in General Pinochet's offices under my direction.

Before going to the Moneda Palace, I gave Frankie the letter for the Supreme Court. I had been carrying it in my attaché case for the last few days, unable to decide if I should mail it, and I asked Frankie to deliver it in person immediately, which he did. I also gave him the telephone numbers Elena had left us in case of dire emergencies. He dropped me on the corner of Calle Providencia at a quarter to eleven. The Italian crew was waiting and we all proceeded to the palace together. The ultimate irony was that I was no longer disguised as a Uruguayan advertising man and wore my own jeans and jacket lined with rabbit fur. The foreign crew—Grazia, journalist; Ugo, cameraman; and Guido, sound man—had already had their credentials carefully checked. But the assistants, whose names had also appeared on the application for the permit, were not asked for any identification whatsoever. That took care of my situation. I entered as a grip in charge of the lighting equipment and cables.

We filmed calmly and efficiently for two full days in the custody of three affable young officers who took turns shepherding us around. We examined everything that had to do with the restoration of the building. Grazia had done her homework very thoroughly on Toesca and Italian architecture in Chile so that no one could doubt the purpose of our film. The soldiers were well prepared, too. With the greatest assurance, they lectured us on the history and significance of every chamber in the Moneda Palace and the way it had been restored with respect to the original building, managing prodigies of evasion and circumlocution to avoid any reference to September 11, 1973. The fact of the matter, though, is that, except for traces of Salvador Allende's regime and public walkways, it had been rebuilt with utmost fidelity to the original plans. Some of the entrances had been closed off, others opened, walls knocked down, bricks moved from one place to another, and the entrance eliminated at Morandé 80, where presidents would receive private visits. The changes in public corridors, and entrance and exit doors were so extensive that anybody familiar with the old palace would have been unable to find his way around in the new one.

The officers had a bad moment when we asked them to show us the original Act of Independence, which had been on exhibition for many years in the hall of the Council of Ministers. We knew it had been destroyed in the bombardment, but the officers would never admit it, promising to get us permission to film it later on, and later on, and later on, until we had finished shooting. Nor were they able to tell us what had happened to Don Diego Portales's desk and many other relics of former presidents left over the years in a little historical museum that had been consumed by the flames. Perhaps the busts of all the presidents since O'Higgins suffered the same fate, although it is common gossip that the military government removed them from the gallery where they had always been in order to avoid including Salvador Allende's. The general impression after a complete tour of the palace was that everything had been completely changed for the sole purpose of expunging the memory of the assassinated president.

At about eleven o'clock on our second day in the Moneda Palace we suddenly heard the quick steps of martial boots and the ratting of metal. Our chaperone officer quickly changed his demeanor, brusquely ordering us, with a brutal gesture, to turn off the lights and stop the cameras. Two plainclothes bodyguards planted themselves in front of us with the obvious purpose of preventing any attempt at filming. We had no idea what this was all about until we saw General Augusto Pinochet himself, his face puffy and greenish, on the way to his office, accompanied by one military and two civilian aides. It was a momentary glimpse, but he passed so close that we clearly heard him say as he went by, "You can't believe a woman even when she's telling the truth."

Ugo stood petrified, his finger paralyzed on the trigger of his camera, as though watching his destiny pass by. "If somebody had come to kill him," he said later, "it would have been very easy." Although we still had three hours of work left, no one felt like filming anymore that day.

A Crackpot in the Restaurant

As soon as we finished filming at the Moneda Palace, the Italian crew left the country, without a problem, carrying the rest of the material. That completed exactly 105,616 feet of exposed film. After six months of editing in Madrid, the final version was cut to four hours for television and two for theaters.

Although the original schedule had been met, and theoretically I should have left Chile, Frankie and I stayed on four more days in the hope of making contact with General Electric. As instructed on the telephone, I went to the same coffee shop every six hours for two days. I would sit at a table and wait patiently, reading my copy of *The Lost Steps*, my talisman for flying. At the next-to-last rendezvous, the long-awaited contact, an angelic twenty-year-old creature wearing the uniform of an exclusive school for girls, La Maisonette, arrived and gave me instructions for the next step. I was to be at Chez Henri, a well-known restaurant in Portales, at six o'clock the same day, carrying a copy of *El Mercurio* and a comic book.

I arrived late, having been held up by a political demonstration. A new group for nonviolent resistance had formed on the heels of Sebastián Acevedo's self-immolation in Concepción. The police attacked the group with water cannons, while more than two hundred of them, soaked to the skin, stood impassively against a wall, singing hymns of love. Still deeply moved by the demonstration, I sat at the bar reading the editorials in *El Mercurio*, as the young student had instructed me, hoping that somebody would come over to me and say: "Are you especially interested in the editorial pages?" I was to answer that I was. The person would then ask why and I was to reply: "Because they contain economic information useful to me in my profession." I was then to leave the restaurant and get into a car that would be waiting for me at the door.

I was on my third time through the editorial pages when I felt somebody passing by give me a poke in the back with an elbow. "This is it," I said to myself. I turned to look. It was a man perhaps thirty years old, with big shoulders, slow-moving, on his way to the washroom. I took it for a signal to follow him but didn't because he had not given the password. I kept an eye on the washroom. He came out, retraced his steps, and gave me another poke like the previous one. Now I could see his face clearly. He had cauliflower ears, purple lips, and scarred eyebrows.

"Hi, there," he said, "how've you been?"

"Fine," I said. "Very well."

He sat down on the stool next to me and addressed me with great familiarity. "You remember me, don't you?"

"Of course," I answered. "I sure do."

After a few more exchanges in that vein, I stopped reading the paper, in an obviously expectant manner, waiting for him to give the password. He paid no attention and remained sitting there, just looking at me.

"Well," he finally said, "how about treating me to a cup of coffee?"

"Sure thing, man, with pleasure."

I ordered two coffees but the man at the counter put down only one before us.

"I asked for two," I told him, "one for the gentleman."

"Certainly," the counterman replied, "I'll take care of him right away."

But he didn't serve him. The curious thing was that the man didn't seem to care, and the oddness of the situation increased my nervousness. He put his hand on my shoulder and said, "You know something? I think you don't remember me. Right?"

I decided then and there to get out of the place.

With that, he took out his wallet, extracted a yellowed newspaper clipping and held it up in front of my eyes.

"This is me," he said.

Then I recognized him. He was a former boxing champion, better remembered in Santiago for being permanently punch-drunk than for his past glories.

I asked for the check so that I could get out before the situation developed any further.

"What about my coffee?" he asked.

"Have it somewhere else," I told him. "I'll give you the money."

"You mean you'll give me the money? Don't hand me that crap! Do you think I'm so down-and-out because I was KO'd that I have no dignity left?"

He was yelling now, and eyes began turning in our direction. I took hold of his thick boxer's wrist in my two enormous hands, which I was fortunate enough to have inherited from my father, and squeezed.

"You be quiet now, understand?" I said, looking him straight in the eyes. "Not another word out of you."

Luckily for me, he calmed down as quickly as he had become agitated. I paid in a hurry, went out into the glacial night, and took a taxi to my hotel. I found a message at the desk from Frankie: *I took your bags to 727.* It was the secret number Frankie and I used for Clemencia Isaura's house. The fact that he had taken my luggage there after leaving the hotel in such a hurry was the final sign to me that the circle had closed. I rushed out, changed taxis several times, going in different directions, and reached Clemencia Isaura's house to find her before the television set in her usual state of divine placidity, watching a Hitchcock film.

Get Out or Go Under

According to the message Frankie had left with her, a couple of plainclothesmen had been in the hotel inquiring about us and had made a note of our registrations. The bellhop had told Frankie, who acted as though he considered it some routine matter having to do with the state of siege and of no concern to him. He checked out nonchalantly, asked the bellhop to call him a taxi for the international airport, and said goodbye to him with a handshake and a handsome tip. The bellhop didn't buy it. "I can put you into a hotel where they'll never find you," he offered. Frankie, of course, acted as though he didn't know what he was referring to.

Clemencia Isaura had prepared a room for me and dismissed the maid and chauffeur. While waiting, she had prepared an elegant supper which she served with candlelight, fine wines, and sonatas by Brahms—her favorite composer. Wading through the wasteland of her late-life frustrations, she prolonged our conversation. She could not resign herself to the possibility that she had wasted her time bringing up children to be *momios*, playing canasta with moronic matrons, to end up knitting and watching tearjerkers on TV. At seventy, she had discovered that her true vocation was the armed struggle, conspiracy, and the headiness of audacious action.

"Better than dying in bed with your kidneys rotting away," she said. "I'd prefer to go out in a street fight against the cops with a bellyful of lead."

Frankie arrived the next morning with a different rented

car from the one we had been using. He brought me an urgent message from three separate sources: "Get out or go under." The latter meant going into hiding with no chance of working, and that was unthinkable. Frankie agreed and had managed to get the last two seats on the afternoon plane to Montevideo.

The final-act curtain was coming down. Frankie had paid off the first Chilean crew the night before, with instructions to settle accounts with the others. He had also turned over the last three cans of exposed film to an emissary from the resistance, to be sent out of the country as soon as possible. This was done so efficiently that when I arrived in Madrid five days later, it was already in Ely's hands. Later Ely told me that those last rolls had been brought to the house by a charming young nun exactly like Santa Teresita de Jesús, who couldn't stay to lunch because she had three other secret missions to discharge that same morning before returning to Chile in the evening. Not long ago I learned, through an incredible coincidence, that she was the same nun who had been my contact in the San Francisco Church in Santiago.

I didn't want to leave as long as there was still the slightest possibility of interviewing General Electric, and even though contact had not been made in the restaurant, I telephoned again from Clemencia Isaura's house after breakfast. The same female voice told me to call back in two hours for a final yes or no. I decided that if I got a positive answer before flight time, I would stay in Santiago regardless of the risk. If not, I would go on to Montevideo. Getting that interview had become a question of honor for me. It would be a profound disappointment if I could not finish my six weeks of good and bad fortune with a triumph like that.

The next call I made brought the same response: "Try again in two hours." There were two more chances, then, before the plane left. Clemencia Isaura insisted that we take a highway robber–style pistol her husband used to keep under his pillow to scare off burglars, but we finally convinced her that it wasn't advisable. When the time came to say goodbye, her eyes filled with tears, prompted as much by the realization that there would be no more exciting adventures as by the genuine affection she felt for us. Actually, my other self was staying in Chile. I put my essential, personal belongings in a small carrying case and left with Clemencia Isaura the large suitcase that contained the British suits, the monogrammed shirts with the strange initials, the handpainted Italian neckties, and the deluxe accessories of the most hated man in my life. The only things of his that I kept were the clothes on my back—and I forgot those intentionally three days later in a hotel in Rio de Janeiro.

We spent the next two hours buying Chilean gifts for my children and for friends in exile. I called for the third time from another coffee shop near the Plaza de Armas and the answer was: "Try again in two hours." This time, however, a man answered, gave the password, and told me that if arrangements could not be made by then, they would have to wait two weeks. Accordingly, we set out for the airport so I could make the final call from there.

Traffic was held up by construction in various places, the signs were confusing, there were many detours, and we kept making wrong turns. Frankie and I were both familiar with the route to the old Los Cerrillos airport but not with the route to Pudahuel, and before we knew it, we were lost in a congested industrial section. We went round and round trying to find our way out and were going the wrong way on a one-way street without realizing it, when a *carabinero* patrol car pulled us over.

I got out of the car determined to beat them to the punch, but Frankie spoke first. Dazzling the two officers with the virtuosity of his golden tongue, he gave them no time to get suspicious. He launched into a rapid improvisation about a contract we had come to sign with the Ministry of Communications to set up a national traffic-control network in Chile by satellite. He then dramatized the possibility that the whole project would be in danger of cancellation if we weren't at the airport in half an hour to catch the plane to Montevideo. We were all so confused trying to figure out the quickest route onto the expressway to the airport that the *carabineros* finally jumped into their car and ordered us to follow them.

Two Unauthorized Characters in Search of an Author

We got to the airport, speeding along at seventy miles an hour behind the patrol car, its screaming siren and flashing red lights sweeping the road clear. Frankie rushed to the Hertz counter to turn in the rented car and I ran to a telephone. I called the same number for the fourth time and got a busy signal. After two more tries I got a response, but the woman who answered made nothing of the password and hung up on me in annoyance. I called right back and now the familiar male voice answered, speaking slowly and with sympathy in his tone, explaining, as he had warned, that the next opportunity would not be for two weeks. When I hung up, angry and disappointed, there was half an hour until departure time.

Frankie and I had agreed that I would go through immigration first while he was settling the bill with Hertz so that he could get away and notify the Supreme Court if I should be detained. But at the last minute I decided to wait for him in the nearly empty corridor outside immigration. He was taking much longer than normal and as time passed I felt more and more that I was attracting attention, standing there with my attaché case and two suitcases, plus bundles of gifts. Then a woman's voice came over the public address system, announcing the last call for passengers on the flight to Montevideo. In a panic, I gave Frankie's suitcase, together with a large tip, to a porter and told him, "Take this bag to the

Hertz counter and tell the man paying a bill there that if he doesn't come immediately I'll have to get on the plane without him."

"It would be faster if you went yourself," he said to me.

I then asked one of the employees at the airline counter, "Please, wait two minutes for me to call my friend who is paying his car rental."

"You have only fifteen minutes," she told me.

I ran to the Hertz counter, not caring what kind of an impression I was making. Anxiety wiped out my other self's stiff composure and I was back to being the same impulsive film director I had always been. The hours of study, of endless detail and painstaking rehearsal went down the drain in less than two minutes. I found Frankie quietly arguing with the clerk over the exchange rate.

"What the hell!" I said to him. "Pay whatever it is and I'll wait for you on the plane. We have only five minutes."

Making an all-out effort to calm down, I stepped up to the immigration window. The inspector checked my passport and fixed an eye on me. Unblinking, I met his gaze. He looked at the photograph, then at me again, and I looked right back.

"To Montevideo?" he asked.

"To Mamma's cooking," I replied.

He glanced at the clock on the wall and said, "The Montevideo flight is taking off." I insisted that it couldn't be, so he checked with the Lan-Chile employee, who confirmed that she was waiting for us before closing the flight. Two minutes were left.

The inspector stamped my passport, smiled, and said, "Have a pleasant trip."

No sooner had I passed through immigration than I heard my assumed name being loudly paged over the public address system. Now I had no doubt: this was it. What I had been able only to imagine happening to others was about to happen to me and there was absolutely nothing to be done. I even accepted it with a strange sense of relief. But it was only Frankie paging me—he had left his boarding pass with me. I had to run to the exit again and ask the officer who had stamped my passport for permission to go out, and then I came back with Frankie in tow.

We were the last to board and did so in such a headlong dash I did not realize that, step by step, I was repeating the exact madness I had gone through in boarding the plane to Mexico twelve years before. We took the last two seats on the plane. At this point, I was experiencing the most contradictory emotions of the entire trip. I felt sadness, anger, and the intolerable pain of exile again, but there was also a feeling of great satisfaction that all the people who had taken part in my adventure came out of it safe and sound. I was brought back to the reality that the adventure was not yet over by an unexpected announcement over the plane's loudspeakers: "Will passengers please have their tickets ready for a check that will now be made."

Two inspectors in civilian clothes, who could just as well have been from the government or the police as from the airline, were already aboard. I have flown a great deal but this was the first time I had ever been asked to show my ticket when already on the plane. It could have meant anything. Distressed, I took refuge in the fabulous green eyes of the stewardess who was passing out hard candies.

"Isn't this an extremely unusual procedure, miss?" I asked.

"What can I tell you, sir? It's something that's out of our control."

Frankie, kidding as he usually does when in a tight spot, asked her if she was staying in Montevideo overnight. She came back in the same spirit with the suggestion that he check with her husband, the copilot. As for me, I was at the point that I couldn't bear another minute of the ignominy of having to live inside somebody else. I had an impulse to stand up when the inspector reached me and shout at him, "You can go to hell! I am Miguel Littín, film director, son of Cristina and Hernán, and neither you nor anybody else has a right to keep me from living in my country under my own name and with my own face." But when the moment of truth came, all I did was hand him my ticket as nonchalantly as I could, crouching inside the protective shell of my other self. The inspector barely glanced at it and returned it without even looking at me.

Flying over the pink-tinted snow of evening in the Andes five minutes later, I realized that the six weeks now behind me had not been the most heroic of my life, as I had hoped on my arrival they would be, but what was more important, they were the worthiest. By this time Pinochet, followed by his retinue, would have emerged from his office, passed through the long, deserted galleries with measured tread, and descended the sumptuous, carpeted stairway dragging behind the 105,000-foot donkey's tail of film we had pinned on him. And I thought of Elena with immense gratitude.

The stewardess with the emerald eyes served us a welcome-aboard cocktail and, without our having inquired, informed us, "The authorities thought an unauthorized passenger had slipped aboard."

Frankie and I raised our glasses in his honor.

"From two who did, *salud!*" I said.

Epilogue

At the time of General Augusto Pinochet's 1973 military coup against Salvador Allende's Popular Unity government, Miguel Littín was one of Chile's most renowned filmmakers. In 1970, Allende had appointed him head of newly nationalized *Chile Films*, through (and against) which Chilean filmmakers sought to implement their theories of "popular culture/popular power" by developing new production and distribution methods.

Littín's films often combine an almost surreal lyricism with scenes of ferociously bloody violence and intense political struggle. *The Jackal of Nahueltoro* (1969) and *The Promised Land* (1973), completed in Cuba, are fictional accounts of true incidents in Chilean history and are regarded as among the finest works in the new Latin American cinema. *The Jackal of Nahueltoro* is the story of an illiterate peasant who murders his common-law wife and her five children, and was made, Littín has said, to "denounce a decaying official state." *The Promised Land*, which depicts the establishment and destruction of a socialist republic in the thirties, has often been interpreted as an allegory, and critique, of the Popular Unity years in Chile.

Littín fled Chile after the coup, and has since lived in Mexico and Spain. "One's homeland is where one is born," he said during a visit to New York in 1983, "but it's also the place where one has a friend, the place where there is injustice, the place where one can contribute with his art." His films include *Letters from Marusia* (1976), *Recourse to Method* (1978), and *Alsino and the Condor* (1983), a Mexican-Cuban-Nicaraguan-Costa Rican coproduction that received an Academy Award nomination for Best Foreign Film.

Last May, Littín slipped back into Chile using a false passport. Assisted by five film crews assembled from several countries (including Chile), he traveled for two months throughout the nation, clandestinely shooting twenty-five hours of film depicting daily life under—and opposition to—the dictatorship.

—Susan Linfield
American Film
January–February 1986